It was late August in 2003 when I arrived at my portable classroom on the edge of campus at Peninsula High School in Gig Harbor, Washington, ready to change the world one hour of freshman English at a time.

Based on the countless movies and television specials I'd seen, I knew exactly what to expect. The path to success is rarely the quickest way up the mountain, but that's the point. Difficulties on the journey become teachable moments and promote group bonding. Most of my days would be filled with conversations about big ideas, witty banter with students, and at the end of each lesson, independent learning.

Every morning I would arrive early and go home late, giving my all to make a difference in my students' lives.

And I would record the whole experience for posterity.

It was time to become a magical teacher.

MAGICAL TEACHING

A Memoir

Derek Smith

Only a lot of boys and girls?
Only the tiresome spelling, writing, ciphering classes?
Only a Public School?
Ah more—infinitely more . . .

> — Walt Whitman, "An Old Man's
> Thought of School," *Leaves of Grass*

In some way, a teenager can be—in a play or a movie,
anyway—a metaphor for a grownup, which is a
half-formed person coping with the world.

> — Kenneth Lonergan, interviewed
> by Rebecca Mead, *New Yorker*

Contents

Prologue

The Night before the First Day

I stare at the brand-new khakis and white oxford shirt on my bed and wonder how I, accustomed to flannel pajama pants and sweatshirts, will don this outfit.

I tried it on in the Target dressing room before I bought it. I suppose it fits well enough.

It is the night before the first day of school, before my first day of teaching at Peninsula High. I'm staring at the outfit in disbelief because I was the kid who stuttered and lisped, who fell in love with books to avoid interacting with my peers. How will I now stand in front of a gang of young people and teach five-paragraph essays? What if they are schemers and jerks? What if they ignore my instructions? What makes me think I can go back to high school when I barely escaped high school myself?

But the foreshadowing in the story of how I decided to become an English teacher is clear. Mr. Martin wrote my name on the board in fourth grade for reading *No Coins, Please* when I should have been memorizing multiplication tables. When I was in middle school, I picked up my grandfather's obsession with homophones. I spent most of ninth and tenth grade writing acrostic poetry. When I entered my junior year of college and my uncle asked me what I wanted to do for a living, and I said I planned to write essays and submit them to anthologies, he suggested teaching. I paused.

I paused, and I thought about influential teachers from my past: the linguistics professor who tapped the linoleum with his bike cleats when he was on a roll, the junior English teacher who drummed her red nails on the computer monitor as she entered grades. I remembered Dr. VanderStaay's lesson on glottal and fricative consonants. I remembered the pulse of pride I felt when Ms. DiBartolo pulled me aside and said I had a knack for writing metaphors that made sense on both sides of the comparison. I remembered the morning Mrs. Steele, my third-grade teacher, wore strawberry ice cream cone earrings to school. I asked if I could lick her ears. She smiled and returned to teaching her lesson.

I thought then that maybe I could be like them. I could make high school more tolerable for young people who felt like outsiders. I could make a difference.

I pull on the pants, button up the shirt, and add a belt from my closet. I tug on my brown Rockport shoes and tuck in my shirt. In the bathroom I study myself in the mirror. My eyebrows are dark like my father's. My forehead is high like my mother's. Look at those brown shoes. Look at those eyes. You checkin' me out?

I am your teacher. You are not checking me out.

I feel like I should already be at my classroom desk, my hands folded at my keyboard, head cocked, waiting for the sounds of students gathering outside my door. I see myself reaching up to adjust my collar, gazing at the semi-circle arrangement of desks, the double horseshoes modeled after my mentor Janet's classroom, occasionally pulling a pencil from my coffee mug of sharpened Dixon Ticonderoga No. 2s. I am getting up to open the door.

What will my students think?

This is the teacher who wants to be my friend.

This is the teacher who is crazy about his marker sets.

This is the teacher who won't let me sleep.

This is the teacher who needs help with the A/V cords.

This is the teacher who jumps up and down to reach the handle on the projection screen.

I have seven hours.

I should get to bed, but I'm thinking about what to wear.

FIRST QUARTER

Gigantic Black Holes
That Suck in Smaller Black Holes

I suppose part of me *did* want to excite students with my zany motivational antics and/or impress them with my credible professional style. I'm disappointed I didn't. Every period of the first day contained a progression of activities.

A few minutes before the morning bell, a pale kid in a white T-shirt and nylon jacket walked up. He looked down at his New Balance shoes. I stood at the door, holding out my hand.

"I'm Mr. Smith," I said.

"Okay," he said.

"The directions are on the projector," I said.

"Okay."

Welcome! the screen read. *Find your spot on the seating chart. Take out two sheets of paper and a pencil.* The boy looked at the chart, found his seat, and got out two pieces of paper.

A girl walked up and pointed at her braces as if I knew her. Her friend wore Abercrombie & Fitch stone washed jeans. More students arrived, unzipped their pencil pouches, and pulled out mechanical pencils and keychain erasers.

When the bell finally rang, I walked from the door to the front of the room and waited while the last arrivals opened and closed their binders, many with movie stubs and magazine clippings arranged in the plastic covers. The shuffle of papers faded to a whisper.

"Do you like reading?" I asked, looking at my lesson plan. "Do you like writing? Have you ever used writing to think about your place in the world?"

One thousand one. One thousand two. One thousand three. I wanted to sound invitational and provide enough wait-time for students to answer.

They outwaited me. Unsure of what to do with their attention, I moved on.

"Copy down what I write on the projector," I said. "These will be our class rules."

I shared the rules my mentor Janet had shared on the first day of class during my student teaching. "Behavior is a choice you make," I said before jotting down the first rule—*Be prepared*—and then continuing, "Please bring all of your materials every day."

During second period I looked less at my lesson plan and more at my students. *Work only on class assignments.* "I'm afraid we won't have time for study hall or make-up days this ye—"

"Are you collecting the summer homework?"

Sixty-four eyes stared at a girl in pink sweatpants. I looked at my seating chart. "Ella?"

"EllaMay."

"EllaMay."

"My name. Are you collecting the summer homework?" First period, the other honors class, hadn't mentioned any summer homework. A few minutes later I had thirty-three two-page essays on my desk.

Third period was my planning period, followed by lunch. Students in fourth and fifth periods, the two "on level" freshman English classes, didn't read the instructions on the projector. "Do we have assigned seats?" they asked. "How old are you? Can people be gay in

Texas? When are we gonna change seats? Are you from the Key Peninsula?" I spent ten minutes explaining the seating chart. A third of the students didn't have notebook paper, so I provided paper. Every time I talked about a rule, they talked. Their T-shirts: *I'm kind of a big deal. Do I look like your therapist?*

We went through the rules. Rolling my lesson plan into a baton, I showed them *Be Courteous.* "In this room there are two parts to this rule," I said. "Raising your hand is the first part. Why is it important that we raise our hands?"

"Because we can't hear if we talk at the same time!" three or four students responded.

I stepped out from behind the projector. "Conversations in classrooms have to be different from conversations at home. In classrooms we need sys——" A boy to my right exaggerated my gesturing, his palms facing up as if he were balancing an invisible platter.

"The second part of being courteous," I said, walking toward him, "is to make no unkind remarks. I'll never forget the day Dwayne DuBois called me a fag in seventh grade."

"I have a question about Japan," the boy interrupted.

I kneeled next to him. "Stay after class," I whispered.

"Whose phones are those?" another boy asked, pointing to a wind chime made of cell phone parts hanging from the ceiling. I had made the wind chime over the summer with phones rummaged from a FREE box at a thrift store.

"Chelsea's and Mike's and Hailey's."

I put students in pairs and asked them to interview each other with get-to-know-you questions like, *If you could ask a wise person one question, what would you ask?* and *What is something about you your teachers may not know?* At the end of the period, students brainstormed bonus interview questions and wrote them on index cards along with anything else they wanted to share.

Grant stayed after class.

"What would you like to know?" I asked. He twisted and tugged his puka shell necklace. "Is there anything at all? I'm open to your thoughts if you're willing to share them with me."

"I want to know if businessmen can buy girls' underwear out of vending machines in Japan," he said.

"Were you making fun of how I gesture when I talk?"

"Your hands were swinging."

"Should I keep my hands still?"

"I don't know."

"You and me, we're going to get along," I said, and excused him.

The day was notable, but not notable like the first day of school in inspirational teacher movies. I never walked in after the bell, tossed a leather briefcase on my desk, and asked, "What should we do today?" No students threw paper airplanes across the room or blasted music from boom boxes. No one threw a sandwich. It was weird to write on the overhead projector, to hold Vis-à-Vis wet-erase pens and control the switches. Weird to stand while 1 Vietnamese, 1 African American, and 118 Caucasian students sat in chairs and looked back at me. David nervously buttoned and unbuttoned his leather cuff. Megan intermittently sipped from a thermos. Matt and Mason wore matching *God of War* T-shirts. Farah slept.

I hope my students will remember my assignments the way I remember dissecting owl pellets on a cookie tray and making rock candy crystals on strings tied to butter knives—with clarity and fondness.

Not every activity can elicit groans of engaged disgust or shine with creative spark, but I can be present with my students as much as possible. Janet, a tall woman with hair cropped into points and scarves that seem to double as capes, is good at finding pockets of quietude and focus in the classroom. She listens to students intently, often without blinking. That's how she makes every day special.

I flip through the bundles of index cards.

Do you think you'll be famous? What does it mean to be a good person? Do you want fries with that? Are there gigantic black holes that suck in smaller black holes? If you could ask a person wiser than you one question, what would it be?

I like asparagus. I was in a rollover accident April 15. I've never left the US. I can say the alphabet backwards. I like test days more than regular days. I like high fantasy novels. I want a strobe light in my shower.

Sept. 3

I held out my Styrofoam plate. A gloved hand piled on tortilla chips. A second gloved hand drizzled on cheese. A third hand grabbed an ice cream scoop from a tin full of brown water, dragged it through a vat of pulverized beef, and delivered the scooped contents in a dome-shaped pile on my plate. I shuffled to my left for a helping of butter-scotch pudding.

I was halfway through my second day.

Around me, girls used carrot sticks to draw designs in ranch dress-ing on their lunch trays. A boy showed his friends how to blow up an empty chip bag and slam it onto the cafeteria table. Thongs and box-ers peeked from the tops of jeans above epoxied pebblestone flooring that sparkled like a lake. Everyone shook cartons of chocolate milk and ate pizza sticks and potato spears and chewy pretzels with cheese sauce.

"I want a watch with, like, thirty small watches inside of it," a boy said.

For my lunch I paid $1.75. The teacher in front of me paid $2.75. I think the woman at the cash register thought I was a student.

I walked to Janet's room on the second floor to eat with the rest of the English department. "I can't keep a stapler around for more than a week," Mr. McKinney said as I walked in. Janet blew on a bowl of soup. Elaina authenticated a small stack of paper bathroom passes with a green flower stamp.

Alice listed the students she thought might be this year's sparklers and frequent flyers as she pulled chocolate espresso beans out of a package. Then she turned to me. "How was the first day?"

I picked at the mound of chips and cheese.

"There are so many faces," I said. "It's like I need to stare at them and say their names over and over while they stare back at me."

"The first week is hard," Janet said, "especially when you're new."

"And then the honeymoon ends," Alice said.

While I ate, Elaina told a story about a brown bat with black wings flying through a broken ceiling tile in a colleague's classroom some years ago. The bat, of course, ruined the teacher's lesson, swooping and darting around the room while students screamed and climbed under their desks. I noted that I had five minutes to get to north campus.

With half of my lunch left, I dumped the Styrofoam plate in the garbage and said goodbye.

I didn't think the interview-based partner introductions would take all period. A bunch of students described their partner by describing their partner's cell phone—the phone their partner had or the phone their partner wanted next. Note to self: the activity did not make everyone seem unique and different.

An hour after the final bell, I pulled out behind a new Honda with a Fox Racing decal in the window and drove my silver 1990 Oldsmobile toward the Purdy Bridge, where boys in board shorts lined the railing like seagulls. To my left and right, kayakers nosed in and out of grassy water along a beach. In the distance, men in yellow rubbers walked across flatbeds towed by oyster schooners, pushing shovelfuls of green-gray shells into the water. The boys in board shorts dangled strings of spit from their mouths. In the rearview mirror, I saw the graffiti-covered parking lot of my red brick school.

In some ways I'm like the boys hanging out on the bridge, perched on the railing, about to jump. Until yesterday, I hadn't spent more than a day in a classroom without the company of another adult. A year of teaching is astonishing to see below me, not unlike a bay of water.

I've already jumped, I thought to myself.

Clouds Gather around the Mountain

Sept. 5

Confession #1: I numbered off students to get them into groups, explained the assignment, facilitated their movement to new places in the room, and then felt the pinch of the math demons—four groups of six instead of six groups of four? Six topics means six groups. Shit. Across the room, Adam hit Grant with Grant's arm, saying, "Why are you hitting yourself? Why are you hitting yourself?" Becca examined her make-up in the reflection of her phone. Austin pried the metal strip from a wooden ruler. Josh sniper crawled under a row of desks, moving toward another group. I prepared to raise my voice but didn't know what to say. I remembered a teacher from my past, a substitute maybe, flipping light switches as a tactic for getting students' attention. I walked to the wall and turned off the lights. When the darkened room failed to quell the noise, I flipped the switches back and forth, on and off, like a light show. No effect. Adam hit Grant with Grant's arm.

Confession #2: I'm the bad-with-names teacher. I called EllaMay "Ella" again, and if I don't have the seating chart in my hands, I have no idea who's who.

Confession #3: I let two mean kids question a nice kid about her reading. "What are you doing?" Zach asked Megan, who had finished her work and was reading *The Bell Jar*. "Yeah," David added, snapping and unsnapping his leather cuff. "What are you doing?"

Confession #4: As a result of Confessions #1, #2, and #3, I'm developing a Look. I didn't think I would want or need a Look, but I've developed an unblinking gaze where I glare at the class, my head turned to the side. I stare at the clock. I stare at the kid looking at the clock. I stare at my watch and back at the sea of students, as I examine the nuances of the whites of their eyes.

This is a confession because I never thought teaching would feel like training pigeons to press levers. I have yet to use a whistle, a gong, or a gavel to solicit students' attention, but somehow the Look, the Stink-Eye, the Hairy Eyeball, the Thousand-Yard Stare, whatever we call it, makes me wonder if my classroom will always be more B. F. Skinner than Benjamin Bloom. My students have already trained me to walk to the edge of my box and press levers, flip fucking switches, deploy the Look, etc.

Confession #5: Grant, or someone who sits in Grant's seat in a different period, wrote *Smith is a faggot* on a desk. After school I cried.

Sept. 8

I was The Hand of Authority. I held out my palm. Becca reached into her pocket and pulled out her phone and gave it to me. I tried to act like this would be one more confiscated phone added to a pile of confiscated phones in my desk drawer, but my hand, trembling like a leaf, gave me away. After school Becca said she took so long to give it to me because she thought I was going to break it into pieces.

Sept. 10

If you were a student in Mr. Smith's fifth period today, you drew on the whiteboard and talked with your friends. You grabbed paper clips and rubber bands from the jars up front. You leaned back in your chair and lifted up your desk with your knees. You leaned forward and brought the desk down. You did this until Room N–7 shook. You didn't read or annotate. You scooted forward and backward, side to side, thumping. You did your best to synchronize your rocking with Adam and Grant, the leaders of the rebellion. You stuffed gum wrappers, pink erasers, and Otis Spunkmeyer parchment paper cookie bags into a paper towel tube when it got passed your way.

"You gonna get with the new math teacher, Smith?" Adam asked.

After the final bell, Mr. Smith wrote about fifth period in his journal, mostly in the third-person point of view to distance himself from the scenes in which he regretted not playing a more active role. He transitioned into first-person point of view as time allowed for the gradual acceptance of reality.

As the light outside went orange, Mr. Smith graded the summer homework, a two-page essay on Is Freedom Really Free? in which one student posited, "In America, freedom is really free. Or is it?"

In the margin I wrote, "I'm intrigued!"

I read the "original simile" exercises from yesterday, a fill-in-the-blank: *The clouds gather around the mountain like _____.*

The clouds gather around the mountain like a fat boy on a trampoline.

The clouds gather around the mountain like a group of Down syndrome babies.
Confusing.

The clouds gather around the mountain like ants closing in on a cracker.

The clouds gather around the mountain like exhaust around a '77 Chevy Caprice's tailpipe.

Better.

The clouds gather around the mountain like ten thousand silver lizards waking up from the winter.

The clouds gather around the mountain like it was you who asked the genie for destruction.

Creative comparisons that transcend ordinary life.

On the back of the cards, students described their family members. Brian, whose binder features an "It isn't going to lick itself" sticker, described his mom drinking whiskey on the front porch. Farah, who said "Fuck this" when I gave the assignment, wrote about fixing the brakes on a dirt bike with her dad.

At 6:15 p.m. I went to Target and bought two boxes of granola bars, seven Michelina's frozen entrees, and a bottle of NyQuil. The NyQuil is because when I try to go to sleep I can't stop thinking about how to split students into diverse discussion groups for the Greek mythology unit, our first unit of study.

Sept. 15

We started *The Odyssey*. I gave the honors classes the 560-page Robert Fagles translation of the epic poem in verse. The regular classes got a 172-page visually illustrated edition, *The Adventures of Ulysses*. I told every class we would sail together and find our way to Ithaca so long as everyone used their oar and rowed, rowed, rowed. The honors students weighed the book in their hands and flipped through the introduction. The "regular" kids chortled. "This book is dumb," Adam said. Justin threw his copy on the floor and said, "I ain't reading this."

"We're reading it together," I said.

"You haven't read it?" Justin asked.

"No," I said.

I told Justin the truth. Somehow, I graduated college without reading *The Odyssey*. I also know next to nothing about mythology. I know that planning and scaffolding the unit was a Herculean task— "Herculean" being the extent of any Greek allusions I might be making. I didn't have time to read the books. Justin doesn't know how serious I was when I added, "I'm learning alongside you."

Sept. 18

For the third consecutive day we started class by reading silently for twenty minutes. Yesterday Mr. Beyer, the teacher next door, had his Pacific Northwest history students start class by competing for prizes in interactive review sessions. Today they did an assessment where they demonstrated their knowledge at different learning stations. I know this because my students and I hear every sound through the wall we share with Mr. Beyer's classroom.

I sat with my students and read. I played again in my mind the scene I see during passing time: students hanging out by Mr. Beyer's desk, Mr. Beyer reclining in his leather rolling chair, Mr. Beyer's students gathered around him, laughing.

I looked at the three *WHY? WHY? WHY?* signs above my whiteboard, a visual reminder to think critically about what we do.

Why do I insist on silent reading?

Why didn't I create learning stations for building my students' background knowledge about ancient Greece?

Why did I skip lunch with the English department to eat a Michelina entree in my dark portable classroom?

The Hungry-Man TV Dinner
Wrestling Tournament

I'm starting to feel the rhythm of the schedule. Honors classes are first period and second period, homeroom every other day, planning period, lunch, on-level classes fourth and fifth periods, and journalism club—an after-school activity Principal Pike threw in as a bonus—on Thursdays.

Paton usually arrives fifteen minutes before school, opens his binder, and writes page after page in his ever-expanding adventure.

Class starts. I give an assignment and ask if there are questions.

"How many points is this worth?" an honors student asks.

"I hate busy work as much as you," I say, "and I know you'll produce quality work regardless of the point value."

"You don't know?"

"I haven't decided."

Our school's name for homeroom is Seahawk Hour. We have no intercom in the north campus portables, so students take turns reading the announcements:

"Do you like Italian sodas? FBLA is selling them at lunch on Thursday."

"The application for a varsity letter in community service is due."

"Class T-shirts are ten dollars. Bring your order form and money to the bookkeeper."

Planning period: I enter attendance and straighten the desks. I admire their semi-circle arrangement. I think about the lesson for tomorrow and pick trash off the floor.

After lunch, a fourth period student walks in and asks what we'll be doing for the day. I point to the agenda on the whiteboard.

I give a simplified version of the assignment I gave the honors classes and move around the room to make sure students are writing the homework in their planners.

James asks for a pencil. If I give James a pencil, I think, he will learn pencils are something Mr. Smith keeps in the cupboard for him to borrow.

I give James a pencil.

After school I make popcorn. As the bag spins in the microwave, I look at the thermostat in my room and contemplate my range of control. Is it good to give pencils to students who have none?

I make a to-do list: update behavior forms, fill out the make-up book for absent students, plan lessons, photocopy handouts, respond to emails, enter grades. Some days I feel like I am looking at a wall of fifty-pound fertilizer bags my dad wants me to move from one corner of his hardware store to the other just so he can make room for more fertilizer bags.

Sept. 25

Not good. The boys in fourth and fifth periods spent much of their time in my class today vaulting over chairs, wandering through rows, and opening my cupboards. I thought about changing the seating chart but remembered what Janet told me last year: "Students can choose to behave where we put them." So while I'm ramping up the level of interactivity in the remaining Greek mythology activities, the expectations for the rest of the class are mainly this: stay in your seat and read. I'm hoping the continuity and consistency will lead to an understanding of the rules, a modicum of compliance, and a bit of engagement with *The Adventures of Ulysses*.

The word *sustained*, I explained to fifth period, means reading until the teacher says to stop.

"Today I'm explaining it," I said, "but tomorrow you'll walk into class and start on your own. I'll be somewhere in the room reading too, so let's not interrupt each other."

Brian held Pippa's pencil case hostage between his thighs. "You can have it back," he said. "Take it." Josh shook a pencil between his forefinger and thumb to make it look pliable. I noticed some students keeping their heads down with their arms around their books, as if their chests would turn the pages while they dozed. "Books on desks," I said. "Heads up."

One day fifth period will have a rich conversation about the book. We'll quote from the text and make inferences and predictions, moving from summaries of the plot to opinions about characters to debates about the story's ethical dilemmas and themes. We might at some point touch upon the essentials of human existence because the conversation will be that focused and free.

Sept. 26

In the back of the room, Mason Jones holds a black crayon and colors a Greek mythology trading card for Cronus, the father of Poseidon, Zeus, and Hades. He wears red-and-black flannel and runs a pick through his hair. Mr. Smith sits at his desk answering emails, occasionally jotting down Mason' words.

MASON. Keep looking at the sky, that's what they want. That's what the government wants. Giving us space programs so we forget to look inside . . . Cronus. Own us. Stone us. That's who I'm coloring. The government kills our free will with their policies.

Mason pauses and looks around the room.

MASON. Cronus ate his babies, which is what guys did before condoms, but it didn't work this time because the baby mama wanted to keep her babies and got pissed at Cronus for eating them. Mama said, "Stop eating our babies," but Hades tasted like barbecue, Poseidon tasted like Kool-Aid, and . . . when Mama gave birth to Zeus the first thing she did was put him in a secret room and give Cronus a rock to snack on. She wrapped the rock in a swaddling cloth, hoping Cronus would eat it without looking at the baby's face.

Mr. Smith makes his way through another stack of similes students wrote about mountains. Mason no longer colors his trading card. He rolls the black crayon up and down his desk.

MASON. The rock-in-a-towel method of disguising the baby worked because it hadn't been seen in the movies before. Mama said, "Oh yeah, this rock-in-a-towel baby is baby Zeus, and I want you to eat him, Cronus!" And Cronus swallowed the rock.

TINA. Is that who you have? Cronus?

MASON. It was basically a boulder burrito . . . so of course it made him puke and a bunch of other babies came out too. What's weird is that the babies came out whole and not chewed up or mashed into pieces.

Mr. Smith opens the gradebook and looks at Mason's grades. Signed syllabus: zero. Comparison story: zero. Silent sustained reading: zero.

MASON. But another version doesn't have puking. Version Two says the ache from the rock was so bad the townspeople cut Cronus's belly open like a C-section and the babies came crawling out like spiders with smiley cartoon faces.

TINA. How do you know?

MASON. *God of War*, baby.

TINA. What?

MASON. The satellite on my roof. Hey, Smith, there's a good story about slicing off sex organs we should read. It's related to mytho—

Seeing someone in the doorway, Mason stands up and picks up his backpack. He addresses his friend from across the room.

MASON. What do you think? Do you think Smith would like sex in the golden age?

STUDENT BY DOOR. Yeah.

MASON. I need to poop.

STUDENT BY DOOR. Me too.

MASON. Piggyback deuce?

STUDENT BY DOOR. Yeah.

MASON. Fudge dragon or poop coil?

STUDENT BY DOOR. Fudge dragon.

Students pack up. Mr. Smith reminds students that they should read the assigned chapter of The Adventures of Ulysses *for homework tonight because they "might have a quiz." Mason's crayon and trading card remain on his desk.*

Oct. 5

I can't stop thinking about Principal Pike interrupting my fourth period.

"One thing that concerns me is paper," she said, pulling me aside. "The district is negative about paper. When they had that whole deal at Artondale, all they found was paper."

"Artondale?" I asked.

"Irritants. Students had rashes. You'll have to take this down," she said, sweeping a hand across my classroom. She pointed to the cartoon stick people I found stapled to the ceiling when I got keys to the room and to the "original similes" poster I made a few days ago. "Think of it as uncluttering. There's a lot to look at in here. Could be distracting. I know you'll take care of it."

I didn't interact much with Principal Pike last year during my student teaching. What little I know about her leadership style comes from a few disorganized staff meetings I attended and from the professional development days she led before the start of school. On the first day she led me and six other new hires down a hallway, saying, "We have a dream here at Peninsula High . . . We want to be known. You may not be aware of this, but we almost made *Newsweek*'s Best Schools list." She stopped and leaned on a door. "This is a door," she said. "We keep this door locked on some days and unlocked on other days because we don't want students developing habits."

Returning faculty joined us the following day for a review of the school rules. Someone suggested banning hats, and a man wearing a denim hat with an adjustable cloth strap came to hats' defense. As he talked, Principal Pike reached up and massaged her neck. "What I want us to accomplish today doesn't have to do with hats," she said. "It has to do with rigor, relevance, and relationships. And it's a work in progress."

She asked us to read the school's mission statement in our binders and to think about revisions.

"Again?" Alice whispered.

"I want you to come up with a better mission statement," Principal Pike said, adjusting the neck of her blouse. "Rewrite it if you want. Blow it up and start over."

"I nominate to leave it as is," Alice said, closing her binder. Elaina yawned into her hand.

"If you want to count this toward your PLC or SIP, sign the sheet in the back," Principal Pike said, "and if that's all you have, I'm not going to keep you here when I know you have important work to do in your classrooms. Your class lists are in your boxes."

Most people headed toward the door. Principal Pike stayed to answer questions. At some point she removed one of her clogs. I asked where my classroom was going to be and if I could get a key.

"N-7," she said, scratching her nyloned foot. "A portable."

"Not so portable," a teacher behind me said.

"Where?" I asked.

"No-Man's-Land," Principal Pike said. "That's what the kids call it."

"There are some trailers on the edge of the parking lot the kids call

Neverland," the teacher behind me explained. "That's the part of campus she's talking about."

I need to write tomorrow's lesson and update the make-up book, but I'm alternately staring at the jellyfish-shaped stains on the orange carpet and staring out the smoky Plexiglas windows of my classroom in Nowheresville. Pink petals on a large rhododendron out the window shiver in a breeze. One of the tennis court nets catches and holds an empty Doritos bag along the center line.

Principal Pike cannot ask me to remove paper from my classroom. Teachers in the movies teach in gymnasiums segmented by rolling walls and in basement supply closets with diamond-patterned windows. They make magic happen for their students no matter their room assignments. I've got a square-ish trailer on the edge of campus with plastic windows, and it's worth defending.

Oct. 6

After Murray, the night custodian, came through and emptied the trash and vacuumed, I got a hamburger from Dexter's Drive-In across the street and sat in the parking lot and brainstormed what to say. *Need to sound like a teacher. Parents should feel confident about my abilities.* Half a block away by a roadside tent full of chainsaw wood carvings, a cedar brown bear stood upright staring into traffic.

At 7:15, I stood by the door to my classroom and greeted parents. Inside I heard conversations about bathroom remodels, stylist appointments, Bible studies, and walkathons. At 7:20 I entered the room.

"Welcome to Open House," I said. "Please make sure to sign the clipboard. I'm distributing copies of the syllabus."

A mom in UGG boots held up the clipboard to see who needed to sign in.

"If a child can sit still for three hours and watch a fantasy movie, he can sit for a thirty-minute lecture," I said, reading from my notes. "If she can spot a brand of shoes from across a cafeteria, she can identify an introductory subordinate clause. And if he can memorize football plays for the big game, he ca—"

"I'm wondering," a dad in the back interrupted, flipping through the syllabus, "why you're teaching *Fahrenheit 451*?" I looked up at the cartoons stapled on the ceiling. A stick figure man with a briefcase in the middle of a road and two stick figure children next to a tree looked back at me.

"Ooookay," he said, "maybe you can tell me how your department chooses books. Why are you reading *Anthem*?"

"Freshman English is thematically organized," I said.

"And the themes?" he asked. A mom in a tracksuit pulled her ponytail through the back of her ball cap.

"Mainly, we look at Joseph Campbell's hero's journey, civil rights, and Greek mythology," I said. "*The Odyssey* is one of the most enduring hero's journeys of all time. So we read that. We know parents value cultural literacy, so we read *Fahrenheit 451* along with our study of teen magazines as we examine the prolifera—"

"They read magazines?"

RIIINNNNGGG. The bell rang. The night was structured like a condensed day of school with each class short enough to keep inquiring minds moving. Parents stood up and gathered their things.

"He's like that other English teacher, Elaina Dugan," the father said to his friend on the way out.

Only four or five parents showed up for the on-level classes. Farah showed up with her dad and spent most of the time looking at the floor. I talked about the make-up book and how students can complete missing work after returning from an absence.

At the end of the night I said goodbye to Mr. Beyer next door as he collapsed trifold poster boards of exemplary student work from prior years and tucked them behind his filing cabinet.

I should have stayed in my apartment and finished responding to Greek invocation poems, but I couldn't resist the sun. I pocketed a Little Debbie Nutty Bar, grabbed a cigarette, and headed to a beach a short walk from my apartment.

My rubber sandals slid on rocks greased with foam. Last time I confiscated Nutty Bars from Pippa I returned them at the end of the period. Today she had her hands in her JanSport again. The rings on her solar system earrings went sideways as she leaned out of her desk to pull a wafer from its wrapper. Marissa had a cigarette on her desk next to her binder, as if it were a pencil.

Down the beach, I saw three birds resting on a log, their heads bobbing. Jack Daniels, Jim Beam, and Jose Cuervo.

Pippa, Marissa, and Paton.

I lit the cigarette, inhaled, and coughed.

The other morning Paton told me that his life dream was unwrapping Apple products forever. He said the only way to disrupt the sadness of an already opened Apple product was to have a conveyor belt delivering Apple products continuously.

I shot an industrial poof into the sky.

I took one more drag and went home to grade poems. I tried to catch up on *The Adventures of Ulysses*, but it's the shitty version with no flashbacks. I fell asleep with the book splayed out on my chest.

I opened my eyes and squinted. I rubbed my hair and blinked. Murray leaned on his gray vacuum. His jeans, weighed down with a walkie-talkie, a key ring, and two leather cases, sagged.

"Go home," he said.

"What time is it?" *I was reading Greek invocation poems . . .* I covered my face. I was at school.

He unplugged an extension cord from an outlet. "You have a bed, don't you?" he asked, winding the cord around his arm. "Go home."

Oct. 17

The plan was that after silent reading I would open the door and my brood of fifth-period beagles would run outside and roll on the lawn. Some of them might participate in "The Hungry-Man TV Dinner Wrestling Tournament," an activity Grant has been proposing in hopes we might do "something competitive." Some students might play four square on the tennis courts. Some of them might eat Otter Pops on the bleachers. The class hasn't yet had a focused conversation about a big idea, but many students can now walk into class, sit down, and read—Mini-Field Day is their reward.

Before school, I put two boxes of Otter Pops in the freezer in the teacher's lounge and drew four-square lines on the courts. At the start of fifth period, I sat down with my copy of *The Adventures of Ulysses*.

Derrell, Austin, and Travis walked into class and tossed empty Mountain Dew and Monster cans in the direction of the recycling container. One can went in. "Really?" I asked. Travis patted his baggy jacket, burped, and said, "I've got another."

Andrew rubbed coconut lotion on his elbows. Farah and Laura whispered across a span of three desks.

"This is SSR," I reminded them. "You should do what you know how to do, what you've done all week."

"Do what you know how to do," Brian repeated, punching Sean in the arm. Pippa laughed. Derrell stood up with a clump of tape in his hand.

"Sit down," I said.

Do this activity, I wanted to plead, *and we'll spend the rest of the afternoon acting like children, pushing colored corn syrup through transparent plastic tubes.*

Unwilling to resort to bribery, I got out of my seat and pointed at the board. "'Silent' means you do not talk. 'Sustained' means you hold the silence until I tell you the time is up. 'Reading' means you keep your eyes on the page and do your best to make meaning out of the words." I looked at my watch: eleven minutes since the bell. "Combine these words into one idea, and you have 'Silent Sustained

Reading.' We do this every day."

I looked at Andrew until he stopped rubbing lotion on his elbows. I looked at everyone until they looked down at their books.

I sat at a desk and pretended to read a bad version of a good story about a hero with a grumbling crew.

After eight pages and seven minutes of silence, I saw Josh buffing his desk with an eraser. I read another page before I looked up and saw Derrell pressing three balls of tape into a larger ball. I cleared my throat. "Silence, Derrell. This is your last warning. You're crossing the line." I looked at my book.

"He wasn't even talking."

"WHEN I SAID SILENCE, I MEANT NO COMMUNICATING, NO EYE CONTACT, NO GESTURES, NO EXPRESSIONS. DO NOT LOOK AT EACH OTHER, DO NOT WHISPER, DO NOT READ LIPS, DO NOT USE SIGN LANGUAGE, DO NOT ASK QUESTIONS, AND DO NOT MAKE TAPE BALLS. SIT IN YOUR CHAIRS, AND SHOW ME THE ROUTINES WE—"

I stopped myself because I could tell.

We were about to spend the whole fucking period.

On this.

I Wish My Reach Were Longer

Defenestrate: the act of throwing someone or something out a window.

Don't worry, I didn't. No one breached the Plexiglas. I fell into my rolling chair, rubbed my eyes, and went home and drank nine Bud Lights.

When I tell Andrew and Derrell they're crossing the line, they look around for a line that doesn't exist. I enforce rules sporadically. Sometimes I give warnings. Sometimes I don't. I'm consistent, I guess, in playing my assigned role in the systematic escalation of conflict. I allow teacher-versus-students to be the central conflict even though I'm aiming for teacher-and-students-versus-social-in-justice-and-institutional-inequality. I'm not surprised I feel as predictable as an ASB candidate promising better dances and expanded off-campus lunch privileges.

My apartment has one sink. Dishes dry next to the toilet. A black support beam runs floor to ceiling through the middle of the living room like a stripper pole. Wheels roll over my head because my mother-in-law apartment is underground, beneath my landlord's garage. Sometimes I lie in bed and look at a picture of a trail in Nine Mile Falls where I used to train for track and cross-country. Ten feet under an old man's Cadillac, I dream of bull snakes and wild turkeys by the river.

When I was in ninth grade, I read Louise L. Hay's *You Can Heal Your Life* and journaled the following six sentences: "I am flexible and flowing. I am safe. It is safe to feel. My feelings are normal and acceptable. I am a Divine expression of life. I love and accept myself." I filled two notebooks repeating those mantras.

Here I am at twenty-two, drinking alone on a Friday night and writing about teaching ninth-grade English.

I was lucky to have two mentor teachers during my student teaching, Elaina and Janet. I hear Elaina's voice in my head, saying, "Teaching is great because you get to do it over. You get to try again the next period or the next day."

But yesterday can't be repeated. Janet had a quotation from the Greek philosopher Heraclitus above her whiteboard: "No man ever steps in the same river twice." Do-overs are a child's four-square fantasy. My feelings are normal and acceptable.

Oct. 20

At the start of fifth period I broke out a deck of red, yellow, and green cards cut from construction paper. Students with binders and books on their desks when the bell rang got green cards. Students who were slow to get started got yellow cards. Students who were off-task got red. "Can I have a yellow card? Why do I have a red? Can I trade?"

"These cards confirm the choices you've made," I said.

A few students moved up or down the color spectrum during the period, exchanging red cards for yellow cards or green cards for yellow cards. At the end of class, I stood at the door and collected the cards as students left. Students with green cards were free to go; students with yellow cards waited a minute; students with red cards stayed longer and talked with me. Farah held up a yellow card and said, "This is green." Jay walked past me, saying he never got one. Josh said he had construction paper at home. "We thought you were going to be cool," Adam said.

After school I got my ink pad and fingerprinted the cards, making up new rules as I went. Missing cards are the same as red cards. Stolen or traded cards are equal to red cards.

Better than a tirade, I guess. The Otter Pop Outburst didn't boost my power so much as combust it.

What other rules can I invent to transform school into a game no one enjoys?

Oct. 21

I went shopping at Target in my pajama pants. Britney was on the cover of *Rolling Stone*. I looked up and saw Micaela.

"Hi," I said.

"Um, hi."

After an equally gawky "See you tomorrow," I walked to the kiosk that plays nature sounds. *Dunes, Canyons, and Desert Wind*. On the mural above men's clothing, three guys in tank tops played basketball in orange and yellow evening light.

I bought two collared shirts, shoeshine, and NyQuil. The cashier checked the age on my driver's license. On my way home, the clouds gathered around the mountain like ants closing in on a cracker.

Last fall I spent eleven days on Mount Rainier, backpacking with friends and learning about plants: Indian paintbrush, bear grass, lupine, avalanche lily. For ten days the weather was perfect. Only in the final hours did the clouds gather around the mountain. We struggled to see each other through the mist, but we were always able to see the trail under our feet.

Oct. 22

Whole-group discussion in first (and every) period: Mr. Smith wearing pajama pants. Reading *Rolling Stone*. In Target.

Funny, but not funny enough for me to forgive fifth period for ruining Mini-Field Day or to stop me from bringing it up again. "Friday was out of control," I said. "We did a lot of things we regret. I understand that in some of your classes, you're in charge and that you don't always know how to handle your power." Adam and Brian doodled on their red cards.

"Cards with anything other than my fingerprints on them will be treated as red," I said.

"It's already red," Adam said. I imagined him floating on a rubber tire in the ocean, eating nothing but saltine crackers.

At the end of class we wrote six-word memoirs, inspired by the book of the same name.

> *Oh, snap, that was due today?*
> *I am lost without my Chapstick.*
> *Milk in a cup of oil.*
> *Are you going to eat that?*
> *The highly unorganized metaphorically expository hominid!*
> *Cram everything in the night before.*
> *I wish my reach were longer.*
> *Apparently, I spread feelings of negativity.*
> *Ehh these boys come and go.*
> *Bored, really bored, I'm seriously bored.*
> *Man, I wish I'd done that.*
> *I think I think too much.*

Someone wrote *Daddy, why did you hurt me?* I think it was Farah, but the author left no name.

I emailed Mr. Thompson, Farah's counselor, and described the lesson and told him about the dark spots on Farah's wrists. The last time I emailed Mr. Thompson, I told him I was worried by the way she keeps her head down with her binder in her lap. He never responded.

Laura wrote a six-word memoir for Odysseus. *Emo-dysseus just wants to go home.*

Oct. 23

I fall asleep every night with *The Odyssey* or *The Adventures of Ulysses* on my chest. In the morning I skim what's left and pray I can boomerang questions in class.

"What does everyone else think?" I ask.

The path of least shame requires stepping off the path. For the second half of the book, small groups will teach assigned chapters to the rest of the group.

Look at this teacher copping out, the student in my head says. *He divides a book he hasn't read into chunks so he can cheer for his students from the sidelines. That's not real teaching.*

Oct. 24

Don't blame me. It's Carol Jago's idea. The way Jago describes students teaching Odysseus's journey makes me believe it will work: "I steer students away from certain kinds of student presentations," she writes in *Classics in the Classroom,* "not because they aren't engaging but because experience with them has shown me that they don't result in deep learning or textual analysis. Examples include: (1) a game show format with students handing out candy for correct answers on trivia questions from their book; (2) puppet shows (too much time spent cutting and gluing and not enough spent thinking); (3) poster presentations full of images from the Internet, sometimes unread. The goal of the presentation must always be to deepen classmates' understanding of *The Odyssey*. No points for cute."[1]

"Your job is to teach," I told students, introducing the idea by doing my best impersonation of Jago, "not to put on a show. Every crew member must do his or her part. No more looking to Mr. Smith for the answers."

---

[1] Carol Jago, *Classics in the Classroom* (Portsmouth: Heinemann, 2004), 140.

Oct. 25

Last night I drank three and a half beers and fell asleep around 8:30. I woke this morning to the sound of my landlord's car backing out above me.

A year ago, I was driving north on Fridays to visit college friends in Bellingham. Mia would ask about my student teaching, and I'd say I was working up to full days of instruction. We would bike to the 3-B tavern, drink beers, and wobble home drunk, wailing Radiohead on the dark streets. When we got home, we would stand around the kitchen and eat family-size bags of corn puffs.

I haven't visited Bellingham in months. I have no idea where anyone lives. I hear secondhand that Jason's pranks continue: wrapping our friend's car in American flags, padlocking his bike to another friend's refrigerator, swapping his roommate's shampoo and conditioner with salad dressing.

Given that someone recently snuck into my apartment and replaced my Costa Rican loungewear and Tevas with brown corduroy pants and Rockports, my life could be Jason's pièce de résistance. He's probably the person who asked Principal Pike to give me a portable classroom in Nantucket. He might be the one who keeps putting paper clips in my pocket.

The best prank of all came from my mom, who mailed me a manila envelope containing personal ads clipped from a small-town newspaper, her comments written in the margin. "She sounds interesting!" my mom wrote next to a description of a Young Life leader and elementary school teacher from southern Idaho. "A teacher! Maybe you could follow up?"

Oct. 27

Students are doing a great job teaching *The Odyssey*. The "teachers" arrive before the bell to rearrange the desks and organize materials. I sit in the back and take notes while they lead discussions about the ritual sacrificing of animals, the hospitality that homeowners and land-dwellers should show weary travelers, and the language used by characters from different economic classes. They ask why Odysseus cries on the beach after cheating on his wife, why Penelope remains faithful in the face of infidelity, why war heroes are expected to behave like role models. One group asks, "What conditions make revenge an acceptable path to justice?" Another group ventures into subplot and discusses Telemachus's plight growing up in a single-parent household, connecting his search for a parent to *Star Wars*, *Home Alone*, *Annie*, and *The Lion King*.

Megan stands out in her group, moving away from the speaker every time she calls on someone, creating an invisible arc that catches everyone else in its net.

The next day she hands me a reflective letter I suggested students write but didn't make part of the grade. "I bit my fingernails until they bled while planning that lesson," she writes, "and then I bit the bloody parts."

My fourth and fifth periods are less ambitious. They wear bedsheet togas while acting out chapters from their summarized version of the book. They interview Odysseus in slang. Several groups gave quizzes at the ends of their lessons, a tactic that generally steers conversations toward the memorization of facts.

In fifth period, Adam noticed a timeline from one of the honors classes stapled to the wall. "There are flashbacks?" he asked. I should have paused the lesson to commend Adam's comparison of the two versions and ask why Homer might have started his story in the middle of the action. I should have introduced *in medias res* as a concept and challenged students to find more similarities and differences, but I put my finger to my lips and pointed to the front of the room where four boys mock-stabbed each other with plastic swords.

Oct. 28

Trisha Abbitt: "I notice Sue has failed something called 'Organization' twice now. Sue says it's that she did not have her book open to the right page when you looked at the class. She got 5/10. What should she do to get 10/10?"

Jordan MacMullen: "I saw Marc received another unexcused tardy on Thurs, 9/21. He told me he is unaware of this and doesn't remember being tardy. When he gets a tardy is he made aware, i.e. given a slip or written notice?"

The trend of these emails is to start with facts and end with criticisms disguised as requests for information, e.g. "Celina appears to be missing 2 out of 5 assignments. Do these assignments get returned to students and, if so, how quickly are they returned?"

Julie Tulay starts with questions and ends with a scenario about a nearly straight-A student failing a group project. "Were students graded on this last project as a whole entity?" she asks. "Or were students graded on their individual efforts within the project? Were students of equal skill levels placed together? When a near straight-A student receives a failing grade, and the project value has such a high point rating, it dramatically lowers the grade for the balance of the semester even with extra credit."

Mrs. Tulay,

I'm glad you're interested in Jacob's work. Jacob made an appointment with me yesterday to talk about his learning this Monday at 2:15 p.m. At our meeting, we'll talk about the evaluation criteria for the assignment you mentioned as well as Jacob's growth as a reader, writer, and thinker. I hope Jacob can provide you with detailed answers to your questions after we meet. Thank you for contacting me. It's always good to hear from a concerned parent.

Derek Smith

Oct. 29

Mason is my one black student in a sea of white, and when he shares synopses of sci-fi books, he's also The One Who Reads in a growing syndicate of reluctant readers.

He says Athena is "Odysseus's wet dream" and points out that Hermes's sandals are not "aerodynamically correct." I worry, though, that if he doesn't put more of his observations in writing, he'll fail.

The little work he does is refreshingly poetic. "What is the value of a world choking on the miasma of its own personal desire?" he wrote on a piece of scratch paper. "I want an immaterial world, a true paradise." Because he struggles to hold on to anything I give him, I made a point of asking if he could hold on to the paper so he could keep working on it the following day.

"Sure," he said.

"Will you really?"

"Sure."

"You're agreeing with me, but will you?"

"Can I leave if I say yes?"

Today we wrote poems inspired by *The Adventures of Ulysses*. Mason spent the day comparing Scylla, the sea monster with one human head and six wolf heads, to his mother after she gets home from work. Our conversation was similar to the conversations we usually have.

"Mason, this is great. Have you considered the journalism club? We need creative minds like yours. Also . . . you know what I'm about to say . . . will you bring this back tomorrow?"

"Sure," he said.

"Are you lying?"

"Can't say."

"Will you try?"

"The poem might divorce me and take its babies with it. It might roadie for Metallica on the Sanitarium tour or miss the bus despite the brand-new shoes it got for the exact purpose of running after busses."

Oct. 30

New day. I asked Mason to take out his poem, and he said he didn't have it. "Hooey!" I said. "Look in your backpack."

"It's not there."

"You put it in there. I watched you. What happened?"

"I don't know. I didn't take anything out," he said, picking up his backpack and holding it out. "Check."

Taylor, the cross-country runner next to him, watched me look inside Mason's backpack. I saw crumpled papers, balled-up papers, accordion papers. "What's in here?" I asked.

"Space-time magic."

I set him to work writing a new version of the poem. At the end of class, I stapled his nearly complete draft to the wall above his head. "Right here," I said, angling my body and pressing the stapler three times.

"Aww, man. Everyone's gonna read it."

"Tomorrow we'll improve it based on what they say."

Nov. 1

I dressed as a modern-day Holden Caulfield for Halloween: black hoodie, black T-shirt, G-Star cap, Vans, iPod, and earbuds. For inspiration, I listened to an old Bright Eyes album, *Letting Off the Happiness,* on the drive to work.

"What are you?" Christy asked during first period.

"What?" I asked.

"What *are* you?" she asked, pointing at my headphones.

"What?"

"For Halloween?"

"I can't hear you," I said, throwing my hands up.

Christy shrugged, handed me a make-up assignment, and returned to her seat.

Fourth and fifth periods were spirited. They laughed and laughed at me, dressed like a teen, and I said, "Well, look at you, Harry Potter, Charlie's Angel, plastic knife-in-head man, and blue-haired anime character with a yellow lasso."

After school, I drove two hours to Bellingham for a party. When someone asked why I didn't have a costume, I started drinking whatever people handed me: coffee and Kahlua, a mug of strawberry margarita, vodka. I hugged a bumblebee, a Swiss girl, and a cardboard robot on roller skates.

I woke up this morning with my head in a closet. As I gathered my things, I saw an older woman outside hosing puke off the apartment complex sidewalk.

A few hours later, I was back in Gig Harbor, brainstorming sarcastic sentences I could write to the elementary school teacher my mom thinks I should date. *Do you call yourself Christian and get drunk like me? I can't believe you would put a personal ad in a newspaper . . .*

What I actually wrote:

I teach ninth-grade English in Gig Harbor, Washington. I always check to make sure my on-level students write down the homework assignment word-for-word.

Teaching is weird. After spending seventeen years focusing on the development of my thoughts and ideas, I'm adjusting to the idea of helping other people develop their own. Many of my students need more help than I ever would have thought.

Random truth: other than handshakes from students and a few hugs at a Halloween party, I haven't been touched by another human being in months. Not a prickle or a scratch.

I saw in your ad that you're a Young Life leader. I used to go to church but haven't had the wherewithal or energy for church shopping.

How are things in Idaho?

Derek

Nov. 5

If only Mr. Sanders wouldn't photocopy chapters of the world history textbook and overheat the copy machine with his two-sided packets. If only the walls of my portable classroom didn't leak in the rain. If only my students could keep their backpacks under their desks without worrying about the wet carpet damaging their textbooks. If only more of the toilet stalls in the main building had doors. If only I could grab a paper clip from the paper-clip jar without grabbing an entire garland of strung-together paper clips. If only I hadn't found a dead rat by my door this morning.

I told Principal Pike that a breathing rat making its presence known during class would turn my carefully planned instruction into a game of hot lava.

If only she had said something other than, "I have great faith in your ability to turn it into a teachable moment."

If only I could roll the whiteboard into the ceiling like a garage door and find a full-time barista in a green apron standing there, cupping a vanilla latte like a dove . . . I could deal with Principal Pike.

I like to think I could teach with nothing but a stick and some sand to draw in, but clearly that's not the case. I need circumstances to blame and people to whom I can compare myself. When students tell me how much fun they're having in Mr. Beyer's class, I generally respond by gazing out the door and across the walkway to the Life Skills classroom, where Mr. Walker has already shown *The Truman Show, Gattaca,* and *Space Jam,* and think, *Well, at least I'm doing better than him.*

We don't have intercoms or fire alarms out here in the demilitarized zone of north campus, so when the alarm goes off, we limp along with classwork until someone hears the distant beeping or someone from another wing of the school opens the door to N-7 and yells WE'RE HAVING A FIRE DRILL CAN JUSTIN COME OUT and HOW COME YOU DON'T HAVE A FIRE ALARM.

If only I had known about the fifth-period fire drill before Principal Pike's fourth-period email, I could have prepared for it. Some students stood on their assigned yard lines on the football field while other students—like mine—bounced like molecules from one chain-link fence to another.

Nov. 6

"Fire drills are one of the few times administrators and other teachers see our behavior," I said, pacing in front of my shivering fifth-period class. "The line you're standing on now is our yard line during fire drills. Do not step off this line until I say so. Do not play on your phones. The rules we have in class follow us out here to the field. The next time we have a fire drill, do as you're doing. There will be other students from other classes misbehaving. Ignore them. Do not follow them through the hole in the fence to the smoker's trail. Do you understand?"

They nodded and shivered, and we went back inside.

Nov. 7

I pulled Mason's poem off the wall and asked him to finish it. He said he didn't like it anymore. "That's how writing works," I said. "We work until we do."

"What if it's done, and I don't like it? Working on it will make it better?" he asked.

"You'll find out when you finish."

"Should I polish the doorknobs in a house with a crumbling foundation?"

"Do what it takes . . . are you mimicking me?"

"Sounds like something you would say."

"You have an opportunity to show creativity here. You can take another path up the mountain, but I want you to get it done."

"We're going up a mountain? Can we piss?"

"What? Why?"

"With my opportunity to be creative, I want to pee on top of the mountain."

Writing the exact same thing as yesterday, he said, shouldn't be a journey. He said there were better metaphors for writing. I asked him what they were. He said he'd get back to me.

At the end of the period, he gave me a poem written from Odysseus's perspective. I taped it to the wall above my desk.

Of My Homeland

I am from golden fields
Chubby black olives
Crackling hearths of roasting game
The sea's lullaby of night
I am from sweet blood wine
Smooth blocks of cheese
I am from powerful warships
Swords that are not virgins to the taste of flesh
I am from the great god Athena
Blest be her name for her wisdom
That shields my land
From the eternal scars of war

Nov. 8

At one point I told students that if they're too shy to ask questions, they could put questions in the Question Jar. Today I got my first submissions.

What languages do angels speak? What language does God speak? Does God tailor his tongue to his audience? I got whipped in the junk with a jump rope during PE and need to know!
Mason

More chips? More breaks? Will you offer playing in the rain? Will you play music during class and have rave parties in the front of the room? Say yes to these ideas!
EllaMay

Fifteen Years Later

I stayed six years at Peninsula, teaching freshman English for four years and junior English for two. The school gave me life. My students made marshmallow sculptures representing their dreams. They performed burial ceremonies for dead adverbs. They formed fan clubs for colons and semicolons. They made peanut butter and jelly "compliment sandwiches," each sandwich containing an individual piece of praise tucked into saran wrap. They wrote poems containing math equations and mailed them to a physics professor. They peeled oranges and noticed the tiny plumes of citrus bursting from the pores in the fruit's flesh. They let me smear football eye paint on their cheeks before final exams and pep assemblies. They made origami fortune tellers reframing childhood disappointments as learning experiences. As a group, we flew around the track while pretending to be a gaggle of geese, flapping our arms and honking, in an imperfect V.

My freshmen resisted *The Odyssey* every year. As I suspected, they weren't allergic to paper, as Principal Pike had suggested that first fall. They were averse to unfamiliar stories. With that in mind, I asked students in subsequent classes to study the plot of the hero's journey in beloved books and movies before opening Homer's poem. Students wrote long metaphors about their family members before close-reading epic similes in the story. Believing everyone should act and everyone should analyze, I blended lessons for the honors and on-level classes. Having skimmed the chapter titled "Slaughter in the Hall," students dramatized the bloodshed of the suitors upon Odysseus's return. When the room was thoroughly strewn with foam swords and bodies, we talked about who in the scene should get mercy, who shouldn't, and why. Students went to the book to prove their points.

Over time, I came to expect that when I read aloud to a class from a text and pause for the kind of silence in which I hope meaning might settle across my classroom like dust motes in the light of dusk, a student who detests manufactured profundity will raise his hand and ask, "Will this be on the test?" Or that when I give the writing prompt "Describe a room you do not like to enter," a reluctant writer who didn't choose to take English and barely puts up with it as a general requirement in the first place might write, "I know exactly how I feel about this room." I came to expect these moments because they happened, and I didn't want to be let down if they happened again. Some students wait all year for the right moment to crest.

Once, a surly junior—whose main contribution to our study of Tim O'Brien's *The Things They Carried* had so far consisted of shouting "Ganja!" during whole-group discussions and talking during silent reading about "unlocking crates" in *Counter Strike: Global Offensive*—raised his hand and said, "O'Brien is careful to note the exact weight of each item, giving us a greater sense of what it must have been like to pack and unpack supplies every day while fighting in Vietnam. The level of description overwhelms the reader in the same way the soldiers must have felt overwhelmed by the war. Of course, we haven't discussed the metaphorical weight the soldiers carry, the burdens they carry in their hearts."

I crouched in disbelief, palm over my mouth, shaking my head. Apparently, I crouched too low because my pants ripped down the side, and I had to teach for the rest of the day from behind a folding table with butcher paper taped to the front of it like a sign at a bake sale.

Sitting there, I felt my feet inside my latest pair of Rockport shoes. The day wasn't ruined, I told myself. This wasn't my first year of teaching. I was grounded.

Sometimes people say they feel more grounded, and what they mean to say is that some part of their life used to be hard and now they float around like Pegasus. Teaching for me is hard and will always be hard. The best days exhaust me more than the bad days. But I know now to manage expectations by considering what I've experienced thus far. I know what to expect—the unexpected.

I'm not surprised I occasionally resorted to flipping light switches to solicit students' attention those first few years. Classroom management is still the first thing to knock me off balance, to kick the chair out from under me on any given day. Like most new teachers, I began my career with a handful of behavior management strategies that are described and simulated in college education classes. Like most new teachers, I leaned on my experiences as a student to guide me. I asked myself if my lessons were as good as the lessons Mrs. Steele, Ms. DiBartolo, and Dr. VanderStaay had given my peers and me. I tried to avoid unreasonable rules teachers had enforced for irrational reasons, like Mr. Harris forbidding food in my tenth-grade world geography class while standing in the middle of the room with his cup of coffee, saying, "When you're a teacher, when you have a degree, you can eat and drink in class too," as if degrees granted teachers immunity from spilling. I wanted to do better than Mrs. Evans, the physics teacher who had rarely smiled and who had always covered her windows with posters to stop students from looking outside—withholding natural light never prevented us from daydreaming. I also thought I could do right by Mrs. Wilson, the tenth-grade biology teacher who found herself in the same room as Alex Putman and Alex Vittori. For about a week, the Alexes took turns increasing the temperature on her fish tank whenever she turned her back. By Friday, Copper and Clementine were floating on the surface because other students, including me, were too afraid to say anything. My own classroom, I thought, could be a place where students summoned the courage to speak out against that kind of cruelty.

Rectifying past and present wrongs is more of a private conviction than a long-term management strategy, I know. But that's the point. I didn't have tried-and-true teaching methods back then. I had memories of experiences that were formative to me personally.

I also had Earl.

"Students' moves are not often personal attacks," Earl Beyer reminded me sometime during my second or third year when I told him about the Alexes killing Mrs. Wilson's fish. By then, I was standing around Earl's desk after school along with his students, chatting.

I found myself comforted by the way Earl—who I no longer called "Mr. Beyer"—abstracted situations and let me abstract them to myself. To my principal, I defended my use of paper. To my mother, I defended my pay. To the insecure teenager in my head, I defended my ability to speak in front of people. With Earl, I was able to work through my challenges in real time, usually by way of true-to-life scenarios passed off as hypothetical dilemmas.

Derek Smith stands by Earl Beyer's desk describing a situation.

DEREK. Suppose a girl who spent the period playing five-finger filet with a blue Bic pen raises an ink-spotted hand and asks, "What if I forget to do the homework?" And suppose in response the teacher rolls his eyes and asks, "What if my fingers break and I can't write anymore? What if frogs fall from the sky?" The teacher knows his response wasn't the best, but what should he do? What would most teachers do? How do you not get annoyed by annoying questions?

EARL. I might try talking with the student the next time I see her. I could show the student how trusting her instincts and attempting to answer her own questions is one way to increase her independence—without having to wait for the teacher. I could also just roll with the questions. "Gosh, your questions are right on today. Keep them coming!"

DEREK. I suppose the teacher could do that. But what if the teacher's patience is limited because the teacher already made a mistake that day? What if the teacher noticed a boy who once described himself as "a party person who will always be a party person" doing tricks in his Heelys on the other side of the room, and this was not the first time the boy had tried "powersliding" in class, and the teacher said, "You know No Child Left Behind, the law we're supposed to follow? Not my deal. I can't include you in the group when you're rolling away from us." What should the teacher do then?

EARL. The teacher should apologize to the boy.

Derek and Earl walk down the hall to the copy machine.

DEREK. Suppose a boy colors the front and back of his hands with yellow and green highlighter and stays after the bell to show the teacher his handiwork. The boy rotates his hands back and forth to make sure the teacher sees all that had escaped him during the period. That night, the teacher gazes into his mirror in his underground apartment and whispers "Okay, okay, okay . . ." as if to reassure himself he will be. Will he be okay?

EARL. He'll be okay.

DEREK. It's just that, he can't believe he didn't notice what must have been a full period of hand highlighting. He could change the boy's seat, but he already tried that. He doesn't want class to feel like a round of musical chairs. He doesn't want to spend so much time hunched over his keyboard, dragging boxes from one side of the monitor to the other, trying to solve The Mystery of the Perfect Seating Chart.

EARL. Some teachers believe constant change stumbles on improvement. At some point it's a losing game of Seating Chart Tetris. No configuration will give the teacher or his students total peace.

DEREK. So the teacher should put up with it?

EARL. Working through it is part of the work. I'm happy to have conversations with kids about their behavior. It's a sizable chunk of what we do.

In *Pilgrim Souls*, Sheldon Vanauken describes a great teacher as having that "strange mixture of unbearable sternness and heartbreaking tenderness."[2] Vanauken is describing Jesus's efficacy as a spiritual teacher for followers of the Christian faith and not the narcissism of an educator with autocratic control over teenagers. Yet "sternness" and "tenderness" still top my list of management descriptors I generally value in teachers. For years, I heard Earl's serious-yet-excitable voice through our shared portable wall. He juggled paradoxical qualities with gravitas. He helped me lean intentionally toward balance, and he pushed me toward centeredness. By talking with him and continuing my conversations with Elaina and Janet, I became more aware of my tendency to swing between extremes. I didn't want to be erratic, so I learned to balance dominance and cooperation, to allow spontaneity but minimize volatility, and to stick by reasonable systems while sympathizing with personalities.

At the same time, I learned to be okay being the teacher students needed. Sometimes this was a different teacher each class period or day. One day I was the teacher who drove to school, thinking, "If I played more games with third period, I would bond more with the knuckleheads, and everyone would behave better." Another day I was the teacher who announced to fourth period, "Camaraderie comes after compliance," and held the whole class after the bell. Inconsistencies like these used to frustrate me, so when it was part of the

---

[2] Sheldon Vanauken, *Pilgrim Souls: A Collection of Spiritual Autobiographies*, ed. Elizabeth Powers and Amy Mandelker (New York: Simon & Schuster, 1999), 525.

plan, it felt good. When it was accidental or emotionally reactionary, I went next door and talked with Earl.

"On paper I believe highly engaged students are better than overly managed students," I told him, "but here I am, driving across town to buy a bell bracelet to tie to a student who can't sit in his seat."

"Highly engaged students are better than overly managed students most of the time," Earl said.

Most of the time, he said. Earl was careful to avoid absolutes. Days aren't "good" or "bad," he told me. If we're telling the truth, most days blend and blur.

After a few minutes of gritching—griping and bitching—about problem students, we would move on to productive work like planning lessons and grading.

These days, I'm more confident about the technicalities of teaching, but I'm also more open to the possibility that my instructional style isn't a match for every student and isn't going to align with other teachers' visions for good teaching. Sheldon Vanauken's vision of a good teacher overlaps with my own, but not every good teacher needs to embrace the stern and tender persona. Good teachers adapt their work to their content, their context, and—more than anything—their students. Some teachers are more sarcastic than sincere. Some teachers listen more than they speak. Bad teachers exist, but the spectrum of good teaching is wider than I previously thought. The sense of purpose and mission that came from modeling my teaching after a quotation someone said about Jesus made me good at my craft, but I think it also sometimes made me unbearable to my more seasoned and level-headed colleagues.

At the end of my sixth year at Peninsula, I got a sore throat. Unable to talk, I typed what I wanted to say to my students into a program that projected the words on a screen for the class to see. After months of increasing soreness and headaches, I went to the doctor, where an x-ray showed amorphous fluid gathering behind my ears. I was pre-scribed antibiotics for mono and walking pneumonia.

I drank tea and continued typing and projecting instructions. I whispered "Okay, okay, okay. Okay, okay, okay . . ." under my breath like a spell. I refused to call in sick because I couldn't imagine what my students would do without me. Education is a serious en-deavor, and if teachers mess it up, young people suffer. I didn't see how I could convey the subtle and not-so-subtle specifics of my classes in a plan left on my desk for a faceless substitute to execute. I didn't see how anyone, even if they understood the subtleties, could execute the plan as well as I could. I had my instructional weaknesses, but no one knew my classes as well as me.

I shouldn't have gone to school with mono and walking pneumo-nia, but I told myself I was needed. Without me, how would my stu-dents talk to each other? How would they navigate the lesson? The irony, of course, was that soon enough I would be gone anyway, and it would be less because of the physical sicknesses spreading through my body than because of my savior complex, which had asked me to sacrifice myself for my students—as savior complexes sometimes do—and then disappear.

It was around this time at Peninsula that administrators proposed a new English curriculum for sixth-through-twelfth graders. My col-leagues and I came to call it The Program for short. "We can no longer afford to close our doors and teach our pet projects," one ad-ministrator said. "We know you're not getting paid to be curriculum developers, so we're not going to burden you with that responsibility anymore." If the proposal passed, students would answer questions in workbooks and teachers would read aloud scripted instructions for activities. Teachers who piloted The Program would get new tech-nology for their classrooms like digital projectors.

As nasal spray dissolved the last of the fluid behind my ears, I wrote emails to the English department faculty reaffirming our capacity to be creative and collaborative. "We grow by sharing our expertise with each other," I wrote from my bed. "We don't need corporations compiling ideas for us.

"Imagine you're walking along a beach with your students," I continued. "You call your students over to discuss something you've discovered. Everyone circles around. You do this off and on throughout the year. One day you hear a student, an increasingly independent explorer some distance up shore, call out, 'Come here! Look what I found!' You all rush to her. The student found a flower. 'This is the night-blooming flower I'm named after,' she says. 'My mom says she walked through my grandfather's garden and saw these flowers the night before I was born.'

"Deciding which beaches to fly over and which barnacles to put under the microscope isn't easy," I concluded, "but it's a philosopher's dream, an activist's obligation, and a teacher's job."

The Peninsula School District curriculum committee and the organization behind The Program didn't agree. They saw canned curricula as a way to "free" teachers to focus on what they called "friendly implementation"—a way of saying teachers were in classrooms with students to paraphrase instructions, encourage young people to show "grit" when learning got tough, and grade assignments. And while I understood the value of establishing common standards and developing shared assessments, I couldn't help but think aspects of my work like cheering on young people and synchronizing important lessons with my colleagues were always just part of what I did.

As I cleaned up the pile of tissues next to my computer, I thought about how so much of the literature I had taught at Peninsula featured characters who stood up against unbending power structures. I knew I was no Guy Montag or Winston Smith. Like them, I was dwelling in a world of absolute morality, but my life wasn't on the line. I was sending emails.

When I got back to school, I met with Elaina and Janet, whose support of The Program I struggled to respect. I didn't understand how teachers with vastly different but equally compelling teaching styles could support a program that would inevitably make them more like each other. We talked about our district adopting the curriculum. They said subpar teachers would improve under The Program, and parents and students would no longer be able to say some teachers were too easy and other teachers were too hard. I met with teachers from other schools and heard their perspectives as well.

Still, I swam against the current, and when English teachers across the district voted to adopt The Program a few weeks later, I felt like Copper and Clementine floating to the top of Mrs. Wilson's fish tank.

As the last few weeks of my sixth year of teaching wound down, I gathered empty boxes from the copy room. I went through my file cabinet and packed my lessons. I packed the two black Swingline staplers and samples of student work I would take with me. I left the meter sticks, scissors, and tape dispensers I had fought so hard for. Principal Pike had gone looking for a new job the year before and had found one in the annual shuffling of bad teachers and administrators from one school district to another. Surely I could find one too. I unplugged my projector and wound the cord around the base. I placed it on the back counter next to a stack of transparency sheets covered in notes from lessons I had created for classes that were so, so different.

SECOND QUARTER

I Am Successful Because I Am Hilarious

Nov. 11

When I turned on the projector this morning, I noticed another piece of paper in the Question Jar:

Do you remember when I was looking for poetry topics, and you said to write a poem about all the different kinds of love?

Well, about that. Every time I think I'm done, I find a new kind of love. Like, Way-Back-When Love, I-Love-To-Hate-You Love, Too-Much-Temptation Love, and on and on. Forever. Any tips?

Megan

Nov. 12

This is a three hundred-word essay I am doing in protest for Mr. Smith. I do not feel I should have to take time away from my homework to complete this essay because I happen to have a sense of humor. I was laughing because the kid in class said something I thought was funny. He said the class reminded him of a bee hive, and the teacher would be like the leader bee. But I knew he meant queen bee. I thought that it was really funny that my male teacher was being referred to as a queen. I may have laughed more than you liked, but I still don't see why I would be required to write an essay. School is stressful, and I thought your class was one of the ones that was the most fun. I did not realize you felt having a sense of humor was so inappropriate to the point that you would require me to turn in an essay. I now understand and am sorry I upset you. I do apologize for talking to my neighbors and laughing too much. Thus, I will do my best to see it does not happen again. I am trying hard to catch up since I broke my leg. I have had a really hard time and having to do this essay in addition to that is slowing me down. This year I have done better in my classes than I have ever done, and I want to keep that up. Please accept my apology.

Derrell

Nov. 14

Cameron told Miranda to suck his cock. Cameron and Miranda are on Mr. Thompson's caseload. Since Mr. Thompson hasn't returned my email about Farah, I emailed a different counselor, apologized for inquiring about students outside her caseload, and asked what to do.

Nov. 20

I looked at the rhododendron out the window. It sported soft brown lumps where pink petals used to be. In class today, I advanced on Texting, crouched by Unprepared, circumnavigated Trouble, placated Rebellion, and praised Moderate Success. But I have no descriptions of individual students because what I'm remembering is how much they needed from me rather than what they gave.

If I ever want this journal to be read by people, I'll need to describe students in detail. I'll need to recount their inner traits and outer appearances. I'll need to outline my interactions with A Few Special Characters.

Not today, Satan.

Nov. 23

When Elaina and Janet mentored me during my student teaching, I noticed a few similarities. Students respected Elaina and Janet because they didn't play favorites, and students worked their hardest for them because they recognized their moral authority. Mostly, though, I noticed differences. When students asked how many words a persuasive essay needed to be, Elaina provided a word count. Janet, however, would pause and ask, "How ambitious is your argument?" Elaina assumed responsibility for explaining the purpose of every lesson. Janet waited for students to cross-reference current lessons with prior understandings. Elaina gave directions; Janet gave hints. Elaina explicated; Janet agitated.

I talk with Elaina and Janet as I stare in the mirror and brush my teeth in the morning.

Derek talks with Elaina and Janet as he stares in the mirror and brushes his teeth.

DEREK. All the other teachers are done with rules.

JANET. Why are you concerned with other teachers?

DEREK. Pippa reaches in her backpack for snacks. Marissa gives Austin henna tattoos. Derrell lines the bookshelf with tape balls. Mr. Beyer seems like he is beyond all this. His students hang out with him during break.

ELAINA. It's never too late to reinforce rules. I reinforce rules all year. Why are you comparing yourself to Earl?

DEREK. I'm always comparing myself to Mr. Beyer. And to you and to Janet. And to Odysseus.

Derek talks with Elaina and Janet while water for tea heats in the microwave in the afternoon.

DEREK. Things are better. Students in fifth period used to yell nonsense. Now they yell thoughts. They went crazy during a fire drill, bouncing off the fence and running around, but we had a practice session. They also used to hate *The Odyssey* but—

ELAINA. The Fagles?

DEREK. The honors classes are reading the Fagles. The regular classes are reading the abridged, illustrated version.

JANET. Why can't everyone just read the Fagles?

And while stapling student work to the portable walls on the weekend.

DEREK. I've been dreaming students are protons.

ELAINA. Units of matter.

DEREK. I'm the electron with the negative charge. I don't see why my students and I have to cancel each other out. Why do I think so much about power? Why do I worry about asserting myself? Do I need to be scary? Is it horrible to say I'd rather be liked?

JANET. Yes.

Nov. 24

After school we had a faculty meeting. Principal Pike said projector cords need to be covered by rugs for an upcoming inspection, and Christmas lights and desk lamps need to be removed.

A science teacher in a sleeveless turtleneck asked about microwaves and mini-fridges.

I was preoccupied thinking about the next unit. We had finished *The Odyssey* and *The Adventures of Ulysses*—what now?

"We should take a spelling walk," Celina suggested in fifth period, "where we walk around the school and you say words and we spell them back to you."

"Definitely," Principal Pike said. "Mini-fridges have to go." Someone joked that the doors on the bathroom stalls had been removed for us ahead of time. Principal Pike clarified that the fire department, not the health department, is conducting the inspection, so we don't need to worry about the doors on the stalls. "This inspection is to make sure things run smoothly for me if we have a shooting."

Nov. 26

The English department is trying the Helen Olson method of teaching writing in which students pick their own topics, but teachers precisely regulate the structure and form of the writing. To write a Helen Olson paragraph, students use four pens: blue for the topic sentence or "big opinion," red for an example or a quotation or a fact, green for an additional sentence elaborating on the example or quotation or fact, and black for the concluding sentence. Executed correctly, the Olson method produces paragraphs as chunky and as solid as gas station brownies.

Our first attempt yielded mixed results. The green pens were spotty, and students didn't understand the difference between opinions and facts.

One of the better paragraphs: *I am successful because I am intellectually minded about computers. I built and sold a computer for $600 profit. I can do things most people cannot do on computers. I'm good enough that some people trust me to fix their expensive machinery. I can make a good profit and do what I want to do.*

There are about ten like that. The weak paragraphs, of which there are fifteen or twenty, deteriorate after the first sentence. *I am successful because I am hilarious. I would be more successful if I was attentive. For example, I worked on my assignment. This shows I do what is expected.*

More than one hundred others round out the continuum.

Dec. 1

Mr. McKinney walked into my second period with a portable stereo tuned in to a local sports radio station, set the stereo on a chair by the door, and stood there. After a few minutes, he picked up his stereo and left. The master schedule says Mr. McKinney teaches science fiction during second period, but I've seen him standing on our north campus patio any number of periods, usually sipping from a coffee mug.

The least a teacher should do is stay in his room during class, not gallery walk the campus grounds while his students watch movies.

It's bad to judge a colleague without the whole story, I know, but so long as I'm appointing myself Collector of Evidence for the Committee Responsible for the Elevation of Derek's Self-Esteem by Way of Comparison and Counterexample, I might as well go all the way.

Remember the time I saw the supervisor for the in-school suspension room reading a true crime novel while the kids under her "watch" slept under desks?

Remember last week when I found a dog-eared book of holiday crossword puzzles by the copy machine?

I would never let students sleep. I would never give out crossword puzzles.

Compare me to the lowest end of the spectrum, please.

The real me knows that to feel good about my craft, I have to want to be as good as Elaina, Janet, and Mr. Beyer, and I have to work toward that goal regardless of their praise or evaluation.

But maybe extending myself a little reward for striving, a little acknowledgement that I'm putting in the time, isn't so bad. If Mr. McKinney leaving his students unattended leaves me superficially satisfied, and Elaina, Janet, and Mr. Beyer make me unnecessarily anxious by virtue of existing, I wonder how and when I should celebrate myself for working hard.

After Mr. McKinney picked up his stereo and left, I assigned numbers for group work only to realize I had counted four groups of eight instead of eight groups of four.

Again.

I thought everything was ruined. But then I reassigned numbers and groups, and everything was fine.

Dec. 2

Boys tore advertisements out of *Cosmo, Seventeen, Teen Vogue, Girl's Life,* and *J-14*. Girls got their ads from *Skateboarding, Sports Illustrated, MAD Magazine, BMXPlus,* and *PCGamer*. Students complained about the gender swap, but no one outright refused. Boys ran their fingers up and down glossy pages. Everyone put their ads into self-defined categories—Ads That Disgust Me, Products I Have Used, Products I've Never Heard Of, Products I Cannot Afford, Real People, Fake People. Megan's categories broke my heart: Things That Won't Matter in the Future, Branded Babies, When You Have Nowhere Else to Turn, and Substitutes for Girlfriends.

"Get off my piles!" students yelled over the sound of tearing paper. "Do fashion spreads count as advertisements? Where's the table of contents?" Hopping between piles of ads while handing out paper clips and sticky notes, I answered students' questions with questions: "What do you think? Why would a publisher hide the table of contents?" When Natasha finished sorting ads from *Maxim*, she held only the magazine's spine. We hung it from the ceiling with a sign: *Maxim magazine with the ads torn out.*

Their engagement felt like love.

It was the kind of day I envisioned while taking Dr. Shannon Shoemaker's Educational Foundations class in college. I remember a drizzly day about halfway through the quarter, when a small group of us found out that Dr. Shoemaker smoked cigarettes under the eaves of Old Main after class. After one of us got the nerve to say hello and Dr. Shoemaker gestured for us to join her, we circled around, and Dr. Shoemaker slipped back into the conversation we had started in class, evoking John Dewey, Maxine Greene, Paulo Freire, and other philosophers of education. "Nowadays they call it 'teacher training' instead of 'teacher education,'" she said. "I train my dog. Are you going to train your students or educate them?" As she finished her cigarette, I envisioned myself one day in a classroom of my own, facilitating grassroots learning, occasionally introducing terms on the projector, marker in hand.

Dr. Shoemaker had a way of acknowledging reality and welcoming hope. "There are lots of things wrong in the world and in our schools," I remember her saying, "and we have lots of reasons to be cynical. But we have even more reasons to be part of the solution."

My friend Noel says that Jesus had a class of twelve highly gifted students, and even he had problems.

Today I worked with five classes of thirty and had none.

Dec. 3

Every time a class goes poorly, I hold it against the next class. When two girls in second period empty their purses of blushes, brushes, shadows, shimmers, glitter, and glosses, and a boy brags to his friend about making a PowerPoint for World History with information from *The Mummy*, I remind students that we should all be focusing on choosing an advertisement worthy of analysis. When the braggadocio and conversations about cosmetics continue, I end up holding a grudge against Seahawk Hour, fourth period, and fifth period. "What's wrong with you?" students ask, as if they weren't the ones who had ruined everything the day before.

"You have five minutes to make me laugh," I said to fifth period, hoping they could help me recover from fourth.

Turning his cap to the side, Adam took me up on my offer. He said when he was six and feeding the ducks at the park in the wintertime, a seagull came down and licked his ear and made him throw his whole bag of bread in the air. He threw the bag with such speed that his body went flying and he landed in the pond where the ducks were swimming and he was frozen in place until some lady—

"Your body went flying?" I asked.

"Yeah, and some lady, no, some ooooooooooold woman," he said, "came and saw me frozen like a police chalk outline and lifted me out of the pond and gave me CPR."

Austin, Brian, James, and Andrew slapped their desks.

"Is this true?"

"I swear," he said, holding up a palm. "First kiss."

Farah looked up from her binder and asked if there was tongue. Adam said we wouldn't believe how much tongue it took to bring him back to life.

I couldn't help but laugh.

Dec. 5

I added more incendiary imagery to the collage on the door: the Statue of Liberty holding a can of Coca-Cola, the REI logo carved into the side of the Grand Canyon, the Taco/Liberty Bell. We started class playing "two ways of looking at an advertisement" and wrote thesis statements in blue ink.

This advertisement is selling hair dye but could also be selling self-worth.

This advertisement is selling cell phone cases; it could also be selling individuality.

This ad sells peanut butter but also family values.

We moved onto examples and quotations and facts (red) and comments and elaborations (green). We've used the Olson pens almost every day, and students have come to associate the colors with the types of sentences. They know I keep replacement pens for scratchy or fading pens in the bin up front. This didn't stop Celina from shaking her green pen and saying the pen lady should die.

"Mrs. Olson should not die. She's a person," I said, "but I understand what you're saying. Remember that the pens have very little to do with good thinking and writing. Your brain produces good thinking. We can write green commentary in invisible ink if we want."

"We don't need the pens?" Laura asked.

"This is how we're practicing," I said. "You need the pens, but if you want to temporarily replace your green pen with a different color, that's fine."

"Lick the tip," Brian said. "It helps." Laura brought the green tip to her tongue.

"Slower," he said.

"I'm tired of the way you reference sex in this room," I said.

"I'm just trying to help her write her paragraph."

I gave him the Look and shifted the focus back to students' work. One paragraph was the goal. *This advertisement is selling extreme fitness,* Derrell wrote. *For instance, the NFL players have a glare on their helmets from the sun. This shows that even when things like the weather are harsh, the players are still training and doing their job, and not admitting defeat.*

Becca wrote about cell phone cases. *Individuality suggests you do not want to be part of the crowd but raised above it,* she wrote. *You don't want the same cell phone or cell phone case. You want the best and priciest one.*

In one rambling, ten-sentence paragraph, Jay mentioned color, price, slogan, camera angle, propaganda, and more. If he's going to talk about all that, I told him, he needs a separate paragraph for each.

You can't attempt complexity like that in this class, said a voice in my head. Your ideas must submit to district-provided organizational structures.

Dec. 8

As part of the schoolwide holiday fundraiser, the wood-carving man from Lance-Saw-Lot Carvings sold life-size eagles and Adirondack chairs in the parking lot. Cub Scouts sold tennis ball Christmas ornaments on the front lawn. Inside, ASB officers laid out trays of candy cane fudge. Parents and grandparents roamed the library and gyms. Secret Garden Quilts, Felted Fantasies, and Whidbey Island Woolies displayed homemade goods on collapsible fences. After visiting Elaina at the raffle table, I walked around the event. I bought a hot buttered rum mix and a loaf of eggnog pumpkin bread.

The cheerleaders ran a picture-with-Santa booth in the gym. I saw the walkie-talkie on Santa's belt loop and knew it was Murray, the custodian. His eyebrows crawled like caterpillars over his glasses.

In the auxiliary gym, the pep band played Christmas classics from the '50s and '60s.

I stepped outside and called my dad. I told him about the annual fundraiser and described the wood-carving man and the custodian dressed as Santa. In line with his typical non sequitur–inspired conversational style, he responded by describing the day he walked out of student teaching and ended his short foray into the education profession. His students, he said, wouldn't listen when he gave instructions. "I told them, 'You probably don't want to learn about this, and you probably don't want to do ten-key operations, so why did you sign up for keyboarding?'"

"You said that to your students?"

"The school responded by saying they didn't want me. By then, there wasn't enough money in the world for me to stay."

"So you quit your student teaching."

When he said life is funny like that sometimes, I left the festivities and went home. I worked on some writing. My dad is a fix-it man, always tinkering around the house. People in our community visit his hardware store for parts and advice. They like talking with someone who has a desire to save what other people might dismiss as defective. I can't believe he gave up on his students. To each his own, I suppose. Writing and teaching is how I do my dad's work of fixing what feels irrevocably broken.

Dec. 10

One afternoon last year, Janet walked across the room we shared during my student teaching. She put a hand on a desk and said the name of the student who sat there during fourth period: Antonio.

She skipped a desk and rested her palm: Amy.

She then touched three desks in a row: Samantha, Lydia, and Maddie. She circled the room saying names and touching desks.

"Do you understand?" she asked. I nodded and we moved on, but I didn't understand the lesson my mentor was imparting until six bites through a plate of spaghetti at my aunt and uncle's house a couple of nights later. Janet had said the names of fourth period students who showed up day after day ready to grapple with ideas, engage, and push our class forward. I had complained about the class's apathy, and Janet had recentered the conversation by calling to mind invested individuals. She touched nearly every desk.

I struggle with fifth period. Their neediness is not their fault, but I wish they'd understand that I can't help everyone one-on-one at the same time and that shouting "Mr. Smith!" doesn't help.

I sat on a stool in the middle of the room and gave everyone a compliment. "Farah," I said, "your ability to make every writing assignment meaningful will help you in all your classes." She looked up.

"Travis, your thoughtfulness before speaking is refreshing. Whenever you raise your hand, I know you've got something good to say."

Halfway through the compliment circle I called Marissa "Melissa" and the class cackled and ooooooed.

Annoying.

Fifth period is annoying.

Dec. 12

I updated grades for progress reports, choosing comments from a menu of pre-programmed options: *A pleasure to have in class. Effort to be commended. Attendance needs improvement.* The time was five after six, and the parking lot was nearly empty.

"So much clerical work!" Janet exclaimed, wrinkling her nose, appearing in my classroom unexpectedly. "Makes a room stuffy." She moved a desk to face my desk and crossed her legs, interlocking her fingers on a knee. Sketches of characters from *The Odyssey* lined a side wall.

"Where did you come from?" I asked, fiddling with the height of my rolling chair. "I've been hearing you in my head all day." Her arm reached up and adjusted a tasseled scarf.

"I just showed up," she said. "How are you doing entering grades?"

"Every three weeks is too much," I said. "It's depressing. It's a letter grade and two lines for comments. There's nothing about what students are learning."

"You don't like that?" she asked, tossing one end of her scarf over her shoulder.

I got out of my chair, walked to the front of the room, and wiped off the whiteboard. I thought about the blackboard Janet and I shared during my student teaching last year. Whenever she dropped an eraser on the tray, a cloud circled around it like a ring around a finger. I felt accomplished going home with chalk on my pants after a long day of teaching.

"Are you a hologram?" I asked. "Murray will kick me out if he walks in and finds me conversing with an empty desk . . . and no, I don't like it. Most emails from parents are about grades. I'm sure the conversations are the same at home. 'Why did you get a zero? Why did you get half-credit?' Parents don't even know what the assignment was or what skills students were supposed to learn."

I set the whiteboard eraser on the tray. No chalky cloud, but I noticed a slight breeze. The flap on the air vent clattered. Janet's spiked hair held firm.

"The grade is a starting point for a larger conversation," Janet said, the tassels on her scarf flitting behind her. "I don't see anything wrong with letter and number grades or with mailing progress reports home to parents every three weeks, so long as those things don't diminish our conversations about students' learning." She leaned toward me. "You decide what happens in your classroom. Do you talk about grades every day? Do you talk about points? If you say, 'This is going to be on a test worth two hundred points,' you can't act surprised when the conversation starts and ends with points." The wall behind Janet splintered. Miniscule squares of wine-dark sea poked through. "But if you talk about what you see and hear in the world around you, you'll see how quickly the community in your room joins that conversation."

"Do you think," I asked, "it will stay this way?"

"What?"

"Everything online, everything standardized?"

"Derek," she said, standing up, "one day everything will come full circle, and our grade books will once again be in perfectly broken-in leather folios—like they used to be. One of us will leave our grade book in a coffee shop and curse the world."

She turned and faced the scene behind her. The wall broke fully apart and revealed a sapphire blizzard. The ends of her turquoise scarf looked like arms reaching out to the horizon.

"Are you disappearing?"

Carpet gave way to shoreline. Ceiling tiles broke into flecks of powdery drift. Janet walked a few feet back toward the water. She walked a few feet more. "Do you have to be this dramatic?" I shouted.

"Did you think I'd use the door?" she asked, looking back as the water rolled over her feet. Then she said something else, but I couldn't hear her. The ends of her scarf met the waves, and she was out of sight.

The shore rolled back, the sky folded in, and I was left in my soda can of a classroom.

On the drive home I decided that, starting tomorrow, I'm writing my own progress report comments and mailing them home to students and families. *Nice without ulterior motives. Values quality over timeliness. Speaks mostly monosyllabically but seems nice! Says he is not a poet, but evidence proves otherwise.*

Walking in the Woods
with a Purse and Nice Clothes

For twenty minutes students wrote everything they knew about their
teen magazines. Afterward they worked in pairs and wrote poems.

Advertising
by Becca & Marissa

Tell me it can't be done, I'll do it.
Tell me the goal is too high,
I will leap over it in lace
leggings, a cute maxi,
and strappy hooker heels.

Is there nothing extraordinary about you?
Do you want to be frozen in the cold like us?
Why would we be walking in the woods
with a purse and nice clothes
when it's snowing?

Sweet. Sexy. Flirtatious.
Buy TRESemmé today.
Explosions. Lightning. Chaos.
BUY TRESEMMÉ TODAY.

Be wild, outgoing, sheer, floral.
Cruelty-free, environmentally friendly.
Challenge me, dare me, even defy me.
  But do not underestimate me
  In my Vans Off the Wall.

Dec. 16

This morning I heard teachers in the copy room comparing gift cards from students. One teacher got four Starbucks cards. Megan and Natasha brought me a T-Mobile, a mobile made of tea bags and twine.

"We thought it could go with your cell phone mobile," Natasha said.

"Tea mobile!" I said to Megan and Natasha. "I'm hanging this up."

Stepping onto a desk with a roll of fishing line in hand, I saw up close the cartoon stick figures stapled to the ceiling. The fine print along the bottom of one drawing reads, *I have more respect for Atticus than anyone I've ever met, and he's not even real.*

In fifth period, Farah gave me a paper snowflake made from an old Greek mythology quiz. I hung it up too.

Jan. 3

I grew up in Nine Mile Falls. I teach in Gig Harbor. Both places have suburban developments with houses painted in colors like "gray seclusion" and "warm cognac" and garages filled with wakeboards and sets of golf clubs. Both places have single- and double-wide trailer parks on the outskirts of town with backyard slash piles turned into fire-pits.

I live in Gig Harbor, but I feel about Nine Mile Falls the way Odysseus feels about Ithaca: "I know no sweeter sight on earth than a man's own native country."[3]

I'm in Nine Mile Falls now. Every Christmas my mom balances porcelain angels on the living room mantle as a reminder to my brothers to wrestle, if they must wrestle, downstairs. My brothers are spending this Christmas with their girlfriends, so the house is quieter than usual. I've spent much of my winter break drinking coffee and staring at the custard terra nova tile.

Can someone so young who lives so much in his head have something to offer teens? Can someone who lives so much between the covers of books have something to say about life? Can someone with so little experience speak with authority on the role of the public intellectual? Should someone who evades confrontation really be facilitating formal debates in the metaphorical town square with our country's future citizens? Should a twenty-two-year-old fresh out of college be teaching social skills?

I don't know.

I know I have to give myself time to accrue wisdom the old-fashioned way: by having uncomfortable experiences and learning from them. The process can't be expedited.

I look at the tile. My childhood home is one shape inside the unfathomably complex tessellation of our world.

I like Nine Mile Falls because I know it, because I glide through the hallway to the bathroom in the dark of night. I can look to the farm across the river in late afternoon and know that if I want to work another summer pulling weeds from rows of bluegrass, I can. These comforts help me confront the doubts that creep into my head when I'm standing in a room of high school freshmen, examining their traffic patterns in the carpet.

---

[3] Homer, *The Odyssey*, trans. Robert Fagles (New York: Penguin Group, 1996), 212.

Jan. 5

They wanted to know what I did over break. Stealing imagery from a Billy Collins poem, I told them I stayed at school.[4]

"You stayed here? Like, in this room?"

"I crawled into the back closet and found a portal to Teacher Narnia. I loved it so much I almost stayed, but then I remembered how much I love watching snow fall from our classroom window and came back."

"What else did you do?"

"I taught myself to make paper snowflakes like the one Farah made."

"Did you teach?"

"The wildest lessons."

"Nuh-uh."

"I made a world out of school. Cardstock clouds. Butterflies with hole-punched wings. Birds with spiral-bound vertebrae flying through a college-ruled canyon. Above it all, a construction paper moon and a felted sun."

"Where did you put it? Where did it all go?"

"I rolled up the world and put it behind the filing cabinet."

"Did you miss us?"

"No one made fun of how I talk, but yeah, I missed you."

Jan. 7

Teachers met in the library, and everyone got a binder of handouts and a bag of blue, red, green, and black pens. The English department was thrilled that Helen Olson, the pen lady, was visiting. Elaina said she knew the day was going to be good because there was a basket of the blue creamers next to the coffee thermos on the counter.

Helen stood in the front of the room wearing a paneled blouse.

---

[4] Billy Collins, "The Teacher," *Poetry* (Chicago: Poetry Foundation, 2003), 84.

"Nice of her to parachute in," Alice said.

Helen blew on the mic. "Hello? Hello?" she said, tucking a tuft of frizzy hair behind her ear. "Raise your hand if you've ever thrown away or recycled a stack of students' homework, ungraded."

Teachers looked around, hands half raised.

"You're right to collect everything," she explained, "and you have to read most of it and grade some of it. But heed this advice: always recycle." Elaina and Janet smiled.

"Writing a Helen Olson paragraph," Helen continued, "makes a great bell ringer, do-now activity, entry task, or whatever your administrators are calling the work students do at the start of class when they walk through the door."

Teachers in the back of the room laughed.

"It could also make a great assessment of the objective, standard, 'essential question,' 'enduring understanding,' or whatever your administrators are calling the goal," she said.

I stirred my coffee and looked around for Principal Pike. I wanted to ask what to do about Mr. Thompson, and how I could get help for Farah.

"It could also be a reflective tool, exit slip, or cumulative activity. It could work in any content area, really."

We got out the pens and wrote paragraphs. The English teachers already knew the formula but acted like model students for Helen, the low-level pedagogical celebrity. Faculty from other departments kept saying that the Olson method wasn't what they thought it was—the process was so useful, so practical.

When I finished my paragraph on *Fahrenheit 451*, I sat back and watched Helen. At one point she tripped on the microphone cord. I remembered Celina's comment—*the pen lady should die*—and I imagined Helen's Keds sliding across the library carpet as her microphone flew into the air.

Helen leaves behind an inky proof of life.

Gathering the excess microphone cord in her hand, Helen said we could end the day early if our paragraphs showed adequate understanding of the process.

"Hey," a history teacher in the back yelled out, "besides throwing away our papers, how can we save time?"

"Quit and become an instructional coach," she joked.

Helen can undermine herself, I thought, because she's confident. Her belief in her work is unshakable. The binder we got when we walked in included a list of nonnegotiables for using the Helen Olson method, including "consistency of program outweighs individual teacher preference" and "formula/structure is a place to start for students who need it; some don't need it at all."

We got out almost an hour early. People clapped. Elaina stayed behind to thank Helen for coming. I wasn't sure how I felt about expanding the gas-station brownie method of writing to the whole school, but I followed Elaina's example and thanked Helen for working with our staff with humor.

Jan. 8

Two months ago, I asked Mason to come up with a metaphor for writing. Today he gave me an origami balloon covered in his handwriting and asked me to unfold it. The note is more or less about school.

Mr. Smith,

You asked for a metaphor. High school is like . . . high school. There is no metaphor to compare it to anything else because not even hell is a strong enough adjective to describe this monstrosity of government-funded programs. It is what it is and always shall be . . . high school. In the beginning, I came here expecting the work to be nothing short of easy, and sadly, I was correct. So correct, in fact, I decided I was above the work and had the right to be lazy because, hey, if I really needed to, I could do the work in mere seconds. I have my home computer connected to a welder. I can type instructions on my keyboard and make the machine do what I tell it to do. So there's your note.

Mason

Dear Mason,

That's cool about the welder. Unfortunately, you're failing freshman English and a few other classes. (I checked.)

You probably tell your parents you're bored, that you're failing because the work is too easy. Here's the thing: The not-so-smart kids are bored too. Sometimes school is boring.

When I ask about your homework, you point to your head, like, I got it up here. But do you? Arguing for some unwritten essay by gesturing to your unrealized potential isn't enough. Sure, you've got opinions, but offering proof and explaining yourself is how you show regard for the reality we share. Maybe you aren't bored so much as afraid. You're afraid that if you try after all these years of kicking back and cultivating a genius rep, you'll flounder.

We've had some good conversations, you and I, but school is a text-based institution. I am your teacher, and if you don't submit work showing effort and skill, I fail you.

Am I saying that to get through high school you must prove yourself in every class to every teacher, over and over again?

Yes.

A few tips on how to do that: (1) Submit to my systems. The infrastructure of my class is meant to cultivate your gifts, not to stifle them. (2) Choose to see the assignments I give you as valuable. Not all work is equally meaningful, but deciding to get more out of your work is one way you can get more out of your work. (3) Stay awake. Working with diverse groups of individuals is one of the great virtues of public education, and when you sleep during group work you're basically telling your group members they aren't worth your time.

I'm a teacher because I walked the steps laid out before me and found success in school systems as they existed. Part of my job now, I suppose, is to perpetuate those systems, to indoctrinate young people like you so that you meet the demands of our culture and economy.

Truth is, I'm not sure if there's a place for me in this system either. I dislike conformity. I love wild permutations. You're a bold and singular personality, a 100-watt bulb in a 60-watt socket, and the 50-watt kids are shining because you're doing nothing.

If you see mixed messages in this missive, you're 100 percent correct.
I'm sorry.
Meet me partway?
Mr. S.

It turns out that Mr. Thompson was put on paid administrative leave. Anne, the president of the journalism club, asked if she could write a news article. I said maybe. To her credit, she got an interview with the lead investigator at OSPI, the Office of Superintendent of Public Instruction. After we went over her interview questions, I left her in the classroom next door to work.

Up until now, my job as journalism club advisor has consisted of hanging out in the computer lab after school on Thursdays, editing articles on homecoming royalty and wrestling matches, and brainstorming headlines like "Academic cheerleaders defy stereotypes" and "Busy seniors deserve more parking." Some club members have been selling lollipops to raise money for a full-color print edition. When they need a break from rolling the quarters they've collected, they snack on cookies and scroll through pictures of cats holding machine guns.

I'm glad Anne wants to expand her horizons with a serious topic. I am. I'm not sure that writing a story about an active investigation is a journalistic endeavor I'm equipped to help her pursue, but isn't that my job? To learn what I need to learn to help her?

After Anne shared the allegations, I called the Student Press Law Center and left a message. I'm waiting for them to call me back.

As part of my emphasis on organization in fourth and fifth periods, I handed out fifty-four pieces of blank neon paper and asked students to keep the paper in their binders. Today I collected the paper. The breakdown: twenty-six students had the paper and turned it in, sixteen students didn't know what I was talking about but emptied their backpacks on the floor to look, and twelve students said they needed to go to their lockers.

In the honors classes, I collected sixty-six reading journals, each with about twenty pages of writing. I carried the journals from my classroom to my car. When I got home, I brought the journals inside my apartment. In the morning I carried the journals from my apartment to my car. In the afternoon I carried the journals from my car into Starbucks, where they sat in the padded chair next to me while I read them one by one, doing my best to respond in the margins with comments and questions. In four hours, I got through sixteen journals.

Fifty more to go.

At least that's what I thought at the time.

Now I don't have any more grading to do because the journals are in a white bucket full of water outside my apartment, bleeding a spectrum of color.

The Hallway Philosophy Club

One night during student teaching I stayed up until one o'clock grading poetry chapbooks. The following morning, Janet rifled through the stack and held up two chapbooks. "What would you say," she asked, "if these two students approached you and wanted to know why their grades were different?" When I hesitated, Janet picked up the stack of chapbooks, handed it to me, and told me to reconsider my grading. She taught me to be careful when assessing student work, and I'm feeling the weight of her convictions tonight.

There's also Mr. Beyer and his Punch Line Posse, the crew who laughs at his jokes between bells and after school.

And Principal Pike wanting things to run smoothly (for her) if our school has a shooting.

No wonder I'm sitting on my mattress, spinning the cap on a bottle of NyQuil and watching a lone carpenter ant look for an opening in the baseboard. I'd like to joke about NyQuil making the voices go away, but I'm guessing this kind of thing is only funny if the jokester doesn't have a problem.

The truth about the journals: I thought about burying them under my landlord's woodpile outside my apartment, but I knew my students would ask about their grades and want to know where the journals went.

I thought about going to a twenty-four-hour coffee shop and staying up all night to get through the work, but the NyQuil on my nightstand didn't like the idea. "Caffeine won't get you through 1,320 pages of writing about independent reading books," the NyQuil said. "There's only so much you can do. If you write one compliment and one question on each journal, you've got twenty hours ahead of you."

"There's only so much I can do?" I replied. "I don't believe that. What kind of teacher says that?"

One of my colleagues jokes about the "margarita curve," a grading strategy for assignments that overstay their welcome in a teacher's home. "Everything's an A by the bottom of the blender," she says.

I spun the cap on the NyQuil. *I'd rather not grade it,* I thought. The dark green color in the bottle reminded me of the ocean, so I grabbed the journals, stuffed them in a paint bucket from my landlord's garage, and walked down to the water.

Clouds gathered around Mount Rainier like cowboys around a campfire. Stars sparkled in dark parts of the sky. I waded out to my knees and pushed down the stack of journals until water rushed into the bucket. When the bucket was full enough to sink below the surface of Puget Sound, I loosened my grip and watched ink swirls rise from the pages like tendrils of smoke.

I work in a service profession where I need to be able to look outward and come up with a vision for my work based on the needs of students. To that end, I've arranged the desks in my room in a double-horseshoe shape so that students can see and converse with each other while facing the front of the room. The truth, however, is that this desk geometry is less important to my students' success than the posture of my heart. I can set up horseshoes and learning stations and other student-centered configurations of furniture, but if I don't believe in creating a community from the ground up, N-7 will be little more than a house of mirrors for my ego.

Conversely, I can stand front and center with my hands on the sides of a lectern and the students staring back at me in lecture-style rows. If I listen to students' questions and comments and respond accordingly, our little satellite station in the North Pole will incubate a sense of community.

I believe I can help create a world where the architecture of the academy expands the chambers of the heart.

But before I devote another sentence to the virtuosic potential of what I might accomplish this year, I should deal with the journals steeping in saltwater outside my apartment.

Jan. 21

"I hesitate to say this because I don't think it's worth telling," I told first period, "and there's no justification for damaging your work."

I told the class I was driving home along the Purdy Spit when suddenly I was overcome with desire to grade their journals outside, next to a driftwood log, if I could find one. I pulled over and walked out to the beach. I sat down and tilted my head to the sun and fell asleep thinking about how far my students had come in connecting their reading to other texts. When I woke up, I saw pages of their journals skittering across the beach and into the water. I ran into the bay to gather as many as I could. When I got back to shore, I found some pages smeared, but I was ecstatic that some of them were still readable.

I looked at the journals heaped on a tarp in my classroom.

"Did you see the sunset?" Katy asked.

"That was why I pulled over in the first place."

"I can't believe you went in the water for us," she said.

"It was the least I could do," I said. "I understand if you are mad at me. I think the words in pencil and ballpoint are okay, but I can't write in the margins like I wanted to."

"Don't worry," Sarah said. "We have hair dryers."

"What happens with our grades?" Evan asked.

"I guess I can erase the assignment in the grade book, or I can give you all As. I don't see any other way."

The subsequent cheering echoed in my mind as I researched ways to maximize my after-school productivity. An article called "Conquer the Paperwork Cougar" gave unoriginal tips like using color-coded bins for In and Out and having students grade each other's assignments.

Jan. 25

I could never be absent. What would I tell the sub?

Dear substitute teacher,

If two football players fold extra copies of Fahrenheit 451 *character development charts into paper footballs and flick them through thumb-and-forefinger goalposts, but they haven't done anything worse, let it slide. My general rule of thumb is to butt in when their harmless games swell to the point of disrupting others or distract them from completing their work. Of course, it's not always easy to tell. If you need to intervene, remember that Adam is the short guy with the backward ball cap, and Grant has the baby goatee. They take two periods of non-optional math—one period to help with homework for the other—and they sometimes leave the daily double with negative feelings. They'll want to know your story.*

If Justin Laroque scribbles on his desk, send him out. He was here every day in September and October, absent most of November and December, and now he's back. Sometimes he scribbles on paper, and as the paper shreds, the pen acts like a drill bit. He keeps going until he's made a small dent in the surface of the desk and his palms are flecked with small pieces of the plastic coating.

You may have to corral a wayward lamb or tell a noisy corner to be quiet, but most students will try. Some of them have PE before English, and since they're running the mile and afraid to shower, they'll be sweaty, smelly, and amped up.

If you use any football or wrestling analogies that work, let me know. My long-distance running metaphors don't seem to be sticking.

Also, Mason has asthma, Jay has a life-threatening allergy to peanuts and

shrimp, Andrew can't have sweets, Josh has trouble getting started, Andrea gets
additional time to work and needs frequent verbal praise, and Brian gets a break
after fifteen minutes. He has a laminated break card for this. Some days he hums
the whole period even when the rest of the room is silent. Matt is 2E, or twice-
exceptional, with Asperger's syndrome and a developmental delay.

Celina has big feelings about school. Her mother is receiving hospice care and
is not expected to survive.

Derek

Jan. 26

Mason and Tristan stopped by fifth period when they were supposed
to be in another class. "Smith," Mason said, leaning against the door
while I was drawing stems for a sentence diagram. "Smith," he repeated. "The Hallway Philosophy Club is here."

"Can you come back? We're in—"

"We just need a minute," Mason said, walking in. "The Hallway
Philosophy Club is an unsanctioned club for students who want an
A. We want an A in everything that cannot be graded and an F in
everything else. We write national anthems for imaginary planets.
Playing the anthems on loop in our heads gives us something to do
at pep assemblies."

"Yeah," Tristan added, "and we don't believe in homework. You
can do homework for fun if you want, but if you turn in anything for
a grade, you're not allowed in. Homework is what we call Everything
Else, and we want an A in that."

"No," Mason said. "We want an A in everything that cannot be
graded. We want an F in everything else."

Farah blew her bangs out of her eyes. Pippa moved a thumb
along a dream-catcher earring.

"If you want to join," Mason said, "you can find me and my partner on the second floor any time."

"Any time," Tristan repeated. "And we accept donations."

Mason surveyed the room. His upturned cheeks pushed his eyes to slits, like cut red grapes. Tristan gave the room a sideways peace sign. Travis, Derrell, and Adam waved back.

The journalism club distributed the full-color newspaper. The Leadership class doesn't love the op-ed piece about doing away with inside jokes on the schoolwide announcements, but the real drama is the front page about Mr. Thompson. "The Board of Directors accepted the resignation of Daniel Thompson, Peninsula High School guidance counselor, on Jan. 20," Anne writes in the news article. "Surrounding his resignation is an investigation of allegations about his behavior." The allegations include simulating oral sex with colleagues and touching female students. A corresponding sidebar breaks down how OSPI handles investigations of educators, starting with documentation of initial suspicions and ending with potential revocation of certificates.

One of the PE teachers confronted me at the copy machine. "I understand that for you this is part of a game, something you do," she said, shaking her head. "But for us this is our life. Kids come and go. We stay."

"Is there an inaccuracy my staff can address?" I asked.

She fixed a bobby pin in her hair and walked away.

When I entered the computer lab after school to debrief the article with the students, Principal Pike was in the front of the room holding the paper up by two fingers, as if it were a dirty sock. "What do you call this?" she yelled. "I call it trash. You think our school needs this?"

"Which parts concern you?" Anne asked.

"I don't have time to make a list," Principal Pike said. "If you don't already know, then maybe I was right. You don't know what you're doing. We'll be talking."

Jan. 29

The descriptive writing prompt I gave: *Compose four snapshots of family members in different areas of your house.*

"Think of it like this," I explained. "A mythological giant lifts the roof off your house and sees your dad in one room and your mom in another room. Your dog is asleep by the front door. You're in your bedroom."

"I live in a trailer," Austin interrupted.

"So?" Becca asked.

"We have two rooms," Austin said.

I thought about Austin throughout the afternoon. Driving home, I passed duplexes, ranchers, waterfront estates, and trailer parks. I imagined Austin talking to his parents.

"He wants you to do what?" his mom might ask.

"Describe our family in different rooms," Austin might reply. "A paragraph for each."

She puts down her book. "Do what you're supposed to. But don't lie."

"He mentioned a dining room."

"Do your teacher a favor," she says. "Write about how all the members of your family hang out in the same room at the same time, a room that does by itself what most people need a bunch of rooms to do."

HINDSIGHT MAN. Why did Mr. Smith give this assignment?

BAD IDEA FAIRY. I told him to.

HINDSIGHT MAN. Did you notice? He's about to pull into a one-room underground apartment.

BAD IDEA FAIRY. We could peek inside. We could give Mr. Smith an assignment. Write one paragraph about eating cereal over the sink. Write another paragraph about watching a candle melt down to a circle of wax.

HINDSIGHT MAN. He won't like that.

BAD IDEA FAIRY. We have to try!

Jan. 30

The Master Mechanic
by Farah
Pat is the father of the household. He is probably working on a Harley Da-
vidson Fat Boy at his new place. There is a problem with the transmission. The
fluid cable is broke, so he tries to fix it with a wrench. When he drops the wrench,
you can see it scatter like a spider running from a rolled-up magazine.

Mad Mom
by Zach
Kristy, the mother, is painting Zach's room a different color. It used to be
peach and now it's dark red. It reminds her of her son's face after she embarrassed
him in front of his girlfriend, which she definitely did.

My Mom
by Antone
When my mom folds clothes it reminds me of pizza boxes stacked on top of
each other behind the pizza place.

My Messy Room
by Adam
The floor looked like someone had driven a monster truck over it. The bed
looked like it had been washed up by the ocean.

Blots of Beethoven
by Christy
The sounds of Chopin echo through the house as Christy practices piano. The
ivory keys are slick and worn. To her, the score makes perfect sense, but to those
who don't play the piano, it looks like gibberish. It is a private and ancient lan-
guage, a language of dust.

David sits at his desk. He straightens the collar on his American Eagle polo shirt and checks to see if his jeans are tucked behind the tongues of his shoes. He snaps and unsnaps his leather cuff. During a break, I ask if he needs help. "I'm fine," he says, looking at me with eyes like holes in trees. I call on him more often. I call on him less often. I call on him the normal amount. I write extra comments in the margins of his work. When I ask how he likes his classes, he says he doesn't know.

"What would you say if you *did* know?"

"I don't know."

I called home as my Michelina's fettuccine alfredo steamed in its cardboard tray. David's dad said he's been helping David. David has no reason to whine, he added. David has everything he could want or need—nice phone, new clothes, college fund.

"He doesn't whine in my class," I said. "He doesn't cause trouble, either. He doesn't smack his lips or string paper clips together, or kick doorstops across the floor."

"That happens?"

"I suppose I'm worried about his apathy more than anything," I said. "He doesn't participate. He turns in enough work to pass, but he rarely shows panache or spark."

"He's never liked English. Do you have ideas on how we can help?"

"If you aren't already having conversations about school, you could try that," I said, looking at my congealing fettuccini. "We could also try tracking his participation each day or week. Normally the behavior form is used for disruptions, but if you or I signed off on it each day, David could see his progress over time. We could reward him for participating and checking in. I have a feeling David sometimes counts on teachers like me devoting their distracted attention to more severe behavior problems. This would help him know we're paying attention."

Dad said he would try.

David is like his dad, I thought. "I'll try" is usually enough.

I'd like David to participate in class because he's excited about learning and not because he's earning a signature on a form or waiting for a new pair of shoes or anticipating a Jolly Rancher on the corner of his desk. I have faith he will one day understand the satisfaction to be found in exploring ideas through literature.

Maybe he'll get there by accident.

Maybe the journey starts with a vision, a form, and a reward.

Feb. 4

Socratic seminar today—a round-table discussion with two rules: don't raise your hand and don't interrupt. Students thought I had gone mad. No hands? No interrupting? How would we talk to each other?

When Elaina facilitated seminars last year, she excused herself from the circle of chairs and tracked the conversation in a notebook. She stayed out of the conversation by giving herself the impossible task of writing it down.

The kids' preparation for today's seminar included reading an excerpt from Neil Postman's *Amusing Ourselves to Death* and answering the question, *To what extent does Sesame Street prepare children for school?* Here's one good moment from each period:

First period

KATY. In a way, the article bugged me. The author was making a judgment, saying all parents do this or all parents do that. *Sesame Street* would be a pretty good thing if you were a single parent.

HOPE. If you grow up in a family without a lot of support, you're going to believe in the power of TV.

JASMINE. But does anyone think *Sesame Street* is educational?

KATY. *Sesame Street* doesn't pretend to be school. Do you see schools anywhere on *Sesame Street*? The street is full of hardware stores and fix-it shops and farmers markets. *Sesame Street* encourages real-life application.

EVAN. *Sesame Street* isn't like school at all. There are no green animals living in garbage cans representing homelessness at school.

Second period

NATASHA. It says here that television demands attention to images.

MIRANDA. Television doesn't demand attention to anything. It has an off button. Children don't have to pay attention when they're watching TV.

JENNA. They don't have to pay attention in school either.

MIRANDA. If they don't want to get in trouble they do.

MEGAN. Television gets a bad rap the way pit bulls get a bad rap.

ELLAMAY. I think it's weird the vampire is the teacher. Does anybody else think that's weird?

Fourth period

TINA. The way he writes about *Sesame Street* makes it corny and stupid. It's not like we have to choose between sitting inside and watching TV or going outside and playing. It's not an either-or.

TAYLOR. He says *Sesame Street* will inhibit our ability to socialize and interact with people. I grew up talking to the TV, so I always felt like I was interacting with someone.

Fifth period

ADAM. Teachers are hesitant to use white paper and black ink because *Sesame Street* is colorful. They photocopy everything on bright paper because they're making up for not having Elmo.

GRANT. You're saying colored paper makes up for not having puppets?

ADAM. I'm saying the show gives kids a false sense of reality.

Feb. 7

"I've got a student pretending he can't read," I said to my mom on the phone. A tea light glowed on my bedroom windowsill next to a picture of Mount Rainier. "He has an IEP that says he has a low reading level, but there's nothing specifying illiteracy. His IEP is full of jargon that I don't understand. He could be telling the truth."

"You're having trouble reading a document about reading? The language should be familiar. You had an IEP."

"What?"

"How do you think you got into speech therapy?"

"You said it was extra help."

"That's what special ed is, Derek. Extra help. I thought we told you."

I sat on my futon. I had an individualized education plan. Outside the window, shadows stretched long across the siding of my landlord's house.

"Did you hear back from the girl in Idaho?" my mom asked. "You're going to love her, I know it."

"Why didn't you tell me?" I asked. "I really can't believe I didn't know."

"We didn't want you making excuses."

"So now you say it was on purpose. Did you have secret meetings behind my back with my teachers? Is that why they never called on me?"

"We didn't tell them not to call on you," my mom said. "We told them you might have trouble responding."

"For how many years?"

"While you were in school."

"The whole time? Most of the time? I'm going to write Idaho Girl a letter and tell her I've updated my personal ad to include the fact that I'm SPED and live in an underground apartment with a stripper pole running through it."

"Derek, we didn't tell you about the IEP because we didn't think knowing about it would help you. We couldn't think of a single way it would help."

I hung up.

"The cat had breakfast early in the morning."

"The cat had b-breakfast early in the m-m-morning," my fourth-grade self repeated. I had said this sentence to myself at home. I didn't know why I couldn't say it to Mrs. French, my speech therapist, or say it the way she was saying it.

"Derek, I know you can do this. I know *you know* you can do this," Mrs. French encouraged. But it was no use. I couldn't say *B*s and for some reason *M*s were giving me trouble as well.

"Start slowly and overpronounce each sound."

I had played a turtle in a local production of *Snow White and the Seven Dwarfs* earlier in the year, a nonspeaking role I was pretty sure the Missoula Children's Theatre staff had invented for sullen children who wouldn't or couldn't speak. I was tired of my mouth standing in the way of what I wanted, so I tried again.

"The cat had ber-eck-fest."

It came out clearly and precisely. Not wanting to risk the rest of the sentence, I stopped. I wondered if Mrs. French would count it.

"Congratulations, Derek. That was the fifth correct sentence."

I knew what came next. When I pressed my way to five, a brown paper bag appeared before my eyes, and the variety of its contents were mine to pick from. Mrs. French let me have two that day, and I selected two packages of Smarties.

After the candy, I left. I suppose Mrs. French wanted to finish on a good note.

I walked into the hallway with my reward, visualizing the end of speech therapy. After that glorious day, I would never again hear intercoms interrupt my teachers and ask me to report to the Specialties Room. I would never again return to class and field questions about where I had been. I would never again disclose the exciting news that I was learning to talk. One day, I imagined, I would fling the whole book of feline feeding patterns into the trash.

I put the Smarties in my nylon lunch bag for the bus ride home and waited for the end of the day.

When the bell rang, I walked with my class single file to the buses. Our names were written in wide-tipped marker on index cards above the windows. I sat next to Holly Allsop, a sixth grader and the only girl in school with a nose ring. I took the window seat, and she stretched her legs in the aisle. I settled in and prepared myself for the ride.

Reaching between my legs, I opened the zipper on my lunch bag and felt around: leftover ham sandwich, juice box, Smarties. I pushed open the middle of a wrapper, took out two of the powder discs, and popped them in my mouth.

"I saw that, Derek."

"Saw what?" I asked, pushing the candy to the area between my cheek and teeth.

"Those candies," Holly said. "Bus Rule Number 7 says 'No Food.' If you don't give me some, I'm going to tell Linda."

My heart pounded. She would tell Linda, the bus driver. Linda wore large sunglasses and enforced every rule of the bus code with no exceptions. She gave out citations and called home if you crossed the street before she gave the signal.

But this was my candy. I had earned it. My vibrating tongue had persevered.

"No."

Holly's reaction was swift. She walked up the aisle and pointed at me. The bus brakes squealed. I zipped up my lunch bag and pushed it to the bottom of my backpack next to my colored pencils. Returning my vision to the line of seats, I saw Linda's hips angling through the aisle, first the left, then the right. I hoped for a misplaced backpack or band instrument to trip her. She would crash. Her sunglasses would break. The bus would evacuate . . . Three seats away, then two, then one. Linda loomed in front of me like a giant.

Her hand appeared, and I knew what it wanted.

I reached into my backpack, pulled out the nylon lunch bag, and took out my Smarties. A yellow and a purple from the open package fell to the floor. The bus was silent.

She turned around and walked back to her seat, my candy in her hand. Everything was blurry. I closed my eyes and rested my head on the window.

My mom took my brothers and me to the public library all the time growing up. We went on weekends, on lazy summer days when we had nothing to do, and after dismissal bells during the school year when she still had errands to run. We would buy White Rain shampoo and Aqua Net hair spray from Kmart and then go to the library. Usually, my mom said we could check out two or three books, but I recognized that as a soft opening bid and regularly left with eight or nine. I felt a thrill walking through the plastic security gate with my arms full, the top book tucked under my chin. I couldn't wait to get home and line up the books by the authors' last names. I couldn't wait to open one, read the first page, and disappear into silence.

Fifteen Years Later

The fall after I left Peninsula, I started work at Renton High School. "You're coming at a good time," the woman in silver hoop earrings said at the top of the stairs in my new building. "The principal who just left . . . we call her tenure The Years of Loose Change."

"Peninsula had a few of those," I said, setting down the box I was carrying. I had bumped into the speech and debate coach by the front entrance. She was showing me the way upstairs.

"We've got new leadership," she said, "and we're going to have a *Dangerous Minds* party to celebrate."

"Where we watch the movie?"

"We watch the movie and take a shot every time Michelle Pfeiffer does something unrealistic, starting with the part where she does karate. The joke is that no one has to worry about embarrassing themselves because it's a party no one remembers."

Later that afternoon as I unpacked boxes, I thought about the *Dangerous Minds* movie and the way Hollywood portrays teachers as urban-slum social workers who transform students' lives in the course of an hour and a half. I thought about the way white teachers on television often have savior complexes, professional and personal impulses that lead them to martyr themselves to rescue students of color. I thought about the savior complex that ended my time at Peninsula, a school with a mostly white student population. I didn't want to fall into these stereotypes or to seem overeager at Renton, but I didn't know what to expect from a so-called "deficit descriptor school"—a low-income, high-minority school where 15 percent of students spoke English as a second language, where the number of students on free and reduced lunch was more than double that of Peninsula.

I turned to a box marked *Good Luck.* Inside, I had placed gifts students at Peninsula had given me when they heard I was leaving: enamel pins shaped like apples and chalkboards, new Sharpie pens, a copy of Scott Westerfeld's *Uglies* with buttercups flattened inside. Additional talismans had mysteriously shown up later on locker clean-out day, the second-to-last day of school, including a toothbrush, a handwritten list of ways students can respond to hallway violence, and a warm ice pack in a Ziploc bag.

I butchered students' names on the first day, calling out Cindy Nguyen's name as "Cindy . . . Nuh-goo-yen?" In another period, Qristiaan walked up to me after I had called Jaivon up to my desk. I said a few sentences to Qristiaan thinking he was Jaivon, and the class busted up, saying, "That's greazy!" and "That's janxy!" I feared that my good luck charms from Peninsula couldn't protect me from my own blunders in this new and unfamiliar world.

I taught my fall transcendentalism unit the way I had taught it in Gig Harbor, asking students to go outside with their spiral notebooks and record their observations.

Fadumo, who had paid the entry fee to a botanical garden, identified fiddleneck, green alder, deer's tongue, vanilla leaf, and red columbine.

What shapes were the leaves? How did they smell? I wrote in her journal.

Bubi wrote that he could *hear Rainier past the powerlines.*

Did you hear birds? Rivers? I wrote back. *What did the mountain sound like?*

The next day Bubi told me he lived on Rainier Avenue and heard cars. He also saw flashing lights outside his window.

Jaivon wrote about revisiting a childhood fortress. He had talked some of his friends into crawling through a tunnel of sticker bushes that led to a mattress with *holes like Swiss cheese, as if someone had spilled acid on it.*

My slowness in adjusting to my new school was not simply because I was committed to lessons that worked in another time and place. I was trying to teach my students ways of being in a classroom that I had learned growing up in Nine Mile Falls, a rural part of the state, and that had been reinforced during my tenure at Peninsula in Gig Harbor. Nine Mile Falls and Gig Harbor were more similar to each other than to Renton.

Over and over that initial year at Renton High, I reprimanded disruptive students who parroted my quips and phrases, mimicked my gestures, or interjected with exclamations. I thought students were being rude when they wouldn't abide by my main rule for polite conversation: one person occupies the floor at a time. "An essential conversational skill," I said, "is the ability to stop and start, a willingness to allow a second or two of silence to pass between one speaker finishing and another speaker starting." I wanted everyone to talk less, so I handed out popsicle sticks representing comments and increments of time in an effort to get students to monitor their contributions. "This is how school works," I said.

My students were of a different mind. They thought arguments could ebb and flow like the tide, crashing against a retaining wall for a while before receding. They thought seminars could have pockets of energy that fizzled and bubbled simultaneously. They thought debates could crescendo and decrescendo like songs and that voices could be concurrent, overlaid upon each other like instruments. They trusted that when people had something to say, they would join in.

These conversational skills—the art of knowing how and when to make an entrance, the necessity of contributing to the inevitable tangling and untangling of a thread, the import of falling in with a group's chorus for a moment even when if sounds like a clamor—weren't lost on my students. They were lost on me. I was the one asking them to move popsicle sticks from one side of their desks to the other.

My students knowing how and when to ignore my instructions was a type of discernment, a demonstration of their ability to prioritize the true goal of our discourse—engagement with ideas. Their insistence was a form of resilience, a testament to their willingness to trust themselves. I saw their conversational style as insubordinate, their engagement as an affront. I didn't know that if my students truly wanted nothing to do with me or with my lessons, they would have ignored me completely.

Renton High had a prayer room in the library and translators available for parent-teacher conferences. The institution sought to serve the particular needs of its student body. I gradually learned to serve my students better by getting to know them and asking, repeatedly, "What am I learning? What—and who—am I seeing in front of me?"

Generally, I learned my students' stories. I learned how their stories differed, and how sometimes the differences among people can bring them together. In addition to English, my students spoke a variety of languages: Cantonese, Vietnamese, Tagalog, Spanish, Somali. When I told them I spoke just one language, they stared at me, a larger separation, in disbelief. I learned how the differences among them increased the value of common reference points in their cultural literacies as well. I rarely saw as much joy on my students' faces as when they collectively pounded on their desks upon finding out that I couldn't Dougie or do the jerk or that I didn't have opinions about Wendy Williams or LeBron.

Many students worked after-school jobs to help out their families.

Some of them worked after-school jobs to conform to the parameters of urban consumption and fashion, to buy the right outfits and head-phones. José, who had picked grapes in 115-degree heat when he was twelve, worked at a smoothie place at the mall. Kurt, who when he was seven had sold packs of *sigarilyos* from a wooden box on the streets of the Philippines, worked at Family Fun Center. They both wore the standard sneakerhead uniform: flat-brimmed New Era 59Fifty cap with the sticker on the brim, studded belt, and Jordans—three parts in matching colors. The Rihanna Navy compared phones on the stairs during lunch. Capitalism and the bullishness of American culture bookended the spectrum of acceptable teenage deviation like it does everywhere. Some of my students liked this, and some didn't. I'll never forget the way Tyler introduced himself on a notecard on the first day of class, as I started my third year at Renton. "I'm the typical Asian guy with the hair that's supposed to be orange but looks more light brown," he wrote. "Don't take this the wrong way, but I don't need English class. I work at my parents' restaurant, but I don't know my grandparents' tea ceremonies. I know some words for family and food, but the reason I'm taking Japanese this year is to make sense of the symbols, to thicken my watered-down culture. That's the class I need."

My colleagues and I worked before and after contract time, replacing professional floobie joobie in our rubrics with language that students would understand: *Bang-up job—this really sings.* Led by a principal with a reasonable philosophy on education—"Shitty school reforms are happening across this country," he said one faculty meeting, "and people are profiting from peddling these silver bullets and theoretical panaceas without knowing the real work involved in transfor-mation"—we dug in. We made students cringe with our list of prepo-sitional phrases: *in the hood, up in here, on the DL, down with that.* We asked students to discuss the role of civil disobedience in democracy and the function of sexualized violence in video games. We discovered what students thought about interracial relationships through in-depth analysis of William Shakespeare's *Othello*. Over the course of the six years I was there, the eleventh-grade English teachers broadened the transcendentalism unit into an exploration of Americana, beginning with Langston Hughes's "Let America Be America Again." Students wrote about objects they considered quintessentially American, like traditional Japanese dresses cut into booty shorts and tiny backpacks and Spalding basketballs and Chevelles on twenty-sixes in the mall parking lot and ukulele covers uploaded to YouTube. I read essay after essay about fresh pairs of shoes: Hyperdunks rotating on the lit-up display at the Nike store, classic low-cut Chuck Taylor All Stars on sale at Champs, and red checkerboard Vans wrapped in tissue paper at Foot Locker.

I walked down the hallway with my silver chain and gold grill, Nakee wrote in his "all-American object" essay, *just cheezing away showing off my silver and gold dentures, girls from left to right going pistachios over me, saying, "Damn, Daddy!"*

Nhu-San, who said she loved many things but ended up throwing away treasures because she never knew if the things she loved were real, ignored the prompt about America and wrote a letter to God instead. *Dear God, may I ask you a question?* she asked. *I'll take the silence as a yes.*

The rules for the *Dangerous Minds* party were as simple as they had seemed: players take a shot whenever something unrealistic happens. From watching the film with a group of friends some years before, I remembered Coolio's sample of Stevie Wonder on "Gangsta's Paradise" and Michelle Pfeiffer's tough demeanor and leather jacket. But I hadn't watched it from the perspective of a teacher.

Gathered around a table of Dixie cups and a skull-shaped bottle of pineapple-infused vodka, we watched LouAnne Johnson have a hard first day with teens from East Palo Alto. The next day the former Marine returned to class and taught the students karate.

Shot.

She updated the curriculum with Bob Dylan lyrics.

Shot.

She tried to protect Emilio from the dangers of the streets by encouraging him to put aside his pride and ask the principal for help.

Shot.

I was probably drunk halfway through the film, but I was still unable to silence my inner voice. Did drinking at unrealistic moments mean we should drink anytime something extraordinary happened? As a group, we hadn't talked about the line between what was real and what was fantastic, what was mundane and what was magical.

My department chair laughed and took a shot when Johnson took her kids to a theme park, but my department chair was the woman who had arranged for every student in the school to see a classical play the year before. I had walked by her class during my planning period and seen her showing students how to power pose.

Mr. Bennett took a shot too, but wasn't he the guy who re-created the world of *1984* in his classroom every spring? He gave students Comrade nametags. He facetiously convicted students of thought-crimes for doubting his edicts. His topsy-turvy methods got students to read the book.

When we paused the film, the choir teacher taught us protest songs to sing at the upcoming school board meeting about budget cuts.

I was hungover the whole day after. But as the rest of the year went by, I kept thinking about the story of the classroom, about how the real and the fantastic might intersect, how fictional characters had pushed me forward during my curriculum battles at Peninsula, how I had left a rural area to teach at an urban school with a desire to do good, and how that's both legitimate and laughably banal.

This is what I came up with: The story of the classroom does not need to be a turnaround tale where a teacher sacrifices everything to rescue a troupe of charismatic youth. It *can't* be. Students are more than vindictive, spoiled brats or tough street kids with tender hearts. Johnson writes about Emilio in *My Posse Don't Do Homework*, the book that inspired *Dangerous Minds*. There, Emilio is more than his masculine image, more than his inability to break through his hard shell.

When I thought of Emilio, I thought of Abdullahi, who had recently opened up to me. Abdullahi rarely spoke, but one day after class we had a heart-to-heart, and he told me about his two brothers, who had passed away when he was younger. He shared a theory about animals and products. "Wild horses don't gallop freely anymore," he said, "so we call the car a Mustang. We remember animals in the names of things. How should I remember my brothers?"

After he left, I looked around my empty room. I thought about my students. When we're together and apart, how should we think about each other? What kinds of impact should the words we use have on the ways we'll be remembered? When I look at table six, Abdullahi's table, I think of his group, who I might describe as dramatically flippant, exuberantly dreamy, and sweetly proud. I might describe the group at table seven as coarsely disgruntled, caustically droll, and mock-heroic. Table eight recently spent part of the period deriding the foreign language teacher who, on the first day of French I, declared, "I'm only going to speak French." She spoke English the first time someone asked to go to the bathroom, Amanda said. I laughed because it was funny and because I remembered the French teacher telling me how nice it had been for Amanda to volunteer to organize her supply cabinet multiple times.

As a writer, I'm suspicious of certain sentences—and stories in general—for the way they ask me to include and exclude details, and thereby flatten reality. Groups of young people are more than their group identities. Individual young people are more than how they present themselves in school. Every young person I write about is more than how I present them on the page. That's true for Amanda, Abdullahi, and everyone in this book.

Just as students shouldn't be reduced to two-dimensional victims or cartoonish criminals, teachers shouldn't be portrayed as implausibly heroic Samaritans or uncommonly ignoble miscreants. Television shows and films don't make this obvious, but teachers are more than superhero saviors, gullible idiots, and unstable opportunists. The complexity of teachers and students alike is what makes telling the story of a classroom a risky and alluring undertaking.

Of course, it's true that on screen and in life, tropes can be based in truth. I've seen building administrators wear Vegas-style ROCK THE TEST! sunglasses while describing the correlation between standardized test scores and neighborhood home values. I've watched teachers in beige Velcro shoes "chaperone" the homecoming dance by setting up a chair by the door and knitting scarves. I've also heard students talk in the hallway like they are characters on TV themselves: "I'm thick, my style is fitted, and this weekend I'm gonna catch a D," as in "I am curvy and well-dressed and ready to spend part of Saturday night having sex."

This doesn't mean we abandon our search for meaningful patterns or that we close ourselves off to individuals or to new ways of reaching every student. Such ways of looking are more important than ever. Classrooms aren't crab buckets in which one crab makes a break for it and then gets pulled down by a culture of low expectations. They are dynamic, evolving biomes. When we do away with our reductive lenses for processing the institution of school and look closely at a single classroom, we see quests, escapes, riddles, and mysteries. We see real-life puzzles that are situated in specific contexts and wrought by time. We see bodies and ambitions in formation, lives caught in metamorphosis, complication, and amelioration. This seeing, when sustained, is powerful, and the power it confers on the people it sees eventually surpasses it.

A classroom can be shaped like an enamel apple pin one day and an ice pack in a Ziploc bag the next. Like my classroom at Peninsula, my classroom at Renton was shaped by my students' personalities. My first year, one of my classes was consistently shaped like a Frito—I never understood it, but Qristiaan had put himself in charge of what he called the Frito Experiment, an investigation wherein he placed a single Frito between the legs of two desks. Every day after I finished taking attendance, Qristiaan would yell, "Frito's here!"

One day I asked Qristiaan if I could see his writing. He shook his head and covered what he had written with his arms.

"Part of my job is reading your writing," I reminded him. His reluctance to write, even as he engaged his peers in class, reminded me of Mason.

He held the paper up to his eyes and said, "I'll read it to you."

After two or three sentences, he lowered the paper, looked me in the eyes, and kept talking. He talked as if the words had risen off the paper and were floating in the space between us. "Are you reading?" I tried to confirm.

"Yeah," he said, "I'm reading."

After three or four more sentences, he got up to finish a carton of macaroni salad over a garbage can. I looked at his paper.

I never really understood what was wrong with Immanuel. He was like an emotionless robot, like his own person in his own world, and sometimes I wonder what is going on in his mind. Maybe he's like a paralyzed kid who doesn't know how to talk or do regular stuff, like brushing his teeth, but as time goes by, he becomes more settled in the teenage life . . . He loves looking at cars, and he stays up all night and hates waking up, and I have to tickle his feet to get him up . . . He loves playing the piano. As soon as he gets off the bus from school he heads to the garage, that's where you can find him. My mom keeps a stock of noodles because that's Immanuel's favorite food, and NOBODY can make him eat what everybody else is eating, even if it's a home cooked meal . . . It's like he's so used to things—if one little thing changes, like his keyboard being on the other side of the garage, he will flip out. I learned from an early age he was going to be more than my mother could handle. His meltdowns sometimes last an hour, but if I'm there I can instantly get him to calm down. In the morning before I wake him up, I have his clothes laid out . . . He's the happiest kid on rainy days. He will stand under the porch and watch the rain hit the ground for hours, or he will be in the rain flapping his hands. He has his favorite song, called "Forever" by T-Pain, and once he hears that, he does his "happy dance." Immanuel's father got killed by a truck, but he has a box on the top of his closet with his dad's picture. One night I was sleeping, and I heard a BANG—Immanuel out-of-the-blue pulled the box down from on top of his closet and tossed it to the door. I'm not sure what that was about, but I sat next to him that night and showed him who "that man" in the picture was, and every now and then, I see Immanuel pull out the box and look at the picture. About four or five years ago, Immanuel started doing this thing where he rubs his chest and touches my arm every time I say a word, and now he won't stop touching my arm when I talk. At first I would get irritated because who wants to get touched every time they talk, but then I got used to it by thinking of it as me being the chosen one.

THIRD QUARTER

The Triangle of Involvement

Two folded papers in the Question Jar, neither of them questions:

> *I like reading even though you smell like whiteboard marker and garbage.*

> *Just so you know, I'm an emotional cinnamon roll.*

I know the handwriting. Jasmine and Evan, respectively.

Normally, David wears polo shirts with popped collars or an Abercrombie & Fitch T-shirt that says something like *Wanna Lift?* Today he wore a black-and-white checkered sweater-vest.

I wore a black-and-white checkered sweater-vest.

"We match!" I said, shaking his hand on the patio outside N-7. "I bet some of your friends think we planned this, but you and I know it's because we have the same taste in clothes." He looked away from me, toward the tennis courts.

"Here's the deal," I said, leaning in. "I'll take off my vest. Do your homework, and I won't mention it. Ignore your homework, and I'll tell everyone."

Excerpt from our first-period Socratic seminar on the potential educational value of video games and the relationship of video games to books.

KEVIN. Some people say reading is isolating, as if reading is for loners. I disagree. I connect with characters when I'm reading.

ALEXIS. Reading is only isolating if for some reason you can't connect, or you can't visualize what's happening.

KATY. I think reading is one kind of learning and video games are another kind of learning. In books you get facts and follow a plot the author created, but in video games you make up the plot yourself.

MARC. And it's sort of the opposite when it comes to settings. Videogames have the setting made up for you while books ask you to complete the setting in your mind.

EVAN. I think over thousands of years of playing video games, people's eyes are going to evolve differently, and we'll have trout eyes we use for squinting.

Almost everyone participated. If I had the full transcript, I'd make copies of it and give it away outside of Dexter's Drive-In to parents and community members who don't believe fourteen-year-olds can be this smart—comically dumb sometimes, sure, but also tragically insightful.

Is it okay to say I don't care about the state test?

My homeroom students are working through a sixty-eight-question Unlock Your Future survey. Most of the questions divide personalities into two types, e.g., *Your desk is (a) usually neat and orderly, or (b) untidy and messy.*

Or: *Are you least likely to (a) waste time not imagining unrealistic possibilities, or (b) waste time avoiding endlessly gathering facts.*

I don't understand that question, and a number of the others, but we tallied our results and went around the room sharing our "career pathways" because that was the Seahawk Hour lesson planned for today.

"Veterinarian," Stephanie said.

"Pediatrician," Shelby said.

"Major in marine biology with a post-bac in electrical engineering," Ross said.

Nick said he's going to test video games before they get released.

Justin, in a long white tee and low-slung jeans, said he's going to have a hot tub full of bitches.

"Responses should reflect 'the real you,'" I repeated from the lesson instructions, "not the way you want to be, think you should be, or are asked to be by someone else."

"Like I said, hot tub full of bitches," Justin repeated.

As the deities of the Greek pantheon would have it, I have Justin for fifth period and Seahawk Hour. He skips a lot, and when he shows up to either class, he throws his backpack from the door to his desk and takes the longest, most circuitous route to get there, usually limping and sipping some elixir of taurine, caffeine, and guarana along the way.

He's the scribbler, and when he's not scribbling, he's sleeping or arguing.

"I think you're describing a lifestyle more than an occupation."

"Get off my jock."

"We're looking for a profession, not a status symbol," I said, looking at the lesson. "I want to know what you want to do for work. Like, auto mechanic, parks and recreation director, freelance animator, stock clerk, interior design—"

"Ringtones make money," Ross said, "and Justin raps. He could write a song that becomes a ringtone."

When I tell Justin or Nick they can't be what they want, I sound like my mom. "How are you going to make money?" she asked me when I told her I planned to major in creative writing. "Engrave your poetry on doorstops and paperweights?"

I thought a sonnet strong enough to prop open doors was a good idea, but I kept my mouth shut, imagining what my mom might say if she found out I had for many years dreamed of being a presenter on stage at the Billboard Music Awards or a dancer next to a float in the Disney Main Street Electrical Parade.

Maybe that's part of it: I'm jealous that Ross and Justin feel so comfortable sharing their outlandish dreams.

Ross thinks Justin can be a ringtone rapper, and the more I antagonize Justin and challenge his plans, the more he'll see me as a naysayer, one of the haters who tell future millionaire rappers they'll never amount to anything. Soon he'll be standing in a snaking line for a talent show audition outside of a convention center, repeating under his breath bombastic lyrics about teachers like me who doubted him.

I'm not here to discourage him. America is Oz, the Land of Make Believe, and there's still time for me to be the poet laureate of doorstops.

Then again, I'm also not here to tell middling students that they're doing magnificently if they're not. Lavishly praising students for easy tasks gives them little reason to then try difficult tasks. My appraisals should be accurate, and no matter what our dreams are—working as a C-squad basketball coach, riding around in a limo with black lights and a hot tub while drinking Bombay Sapphire—we need to articulate a plan and accompany that plan with consistent follow-through.

"If you're serious about it," I said, "write it down."

Feb. 13

"Have you all seen David's black-and-white sweater?" I asked second period. "He's not wearing it, but I'm pretty sure he has the one I'm wearing. If we both wear them on the same day, we'll match.

"But if we're going to have twin day," I said to David, walking toward him, resting my hand on his armrest, offering a subtle insinuation about his uncertain sartorial future in our class, "we need to do it soon."

David leaned forward, grabbed the sides of his desk, and scooted the awkward seat-desk combo to the side. Zach, whose feet had been stretching under David's desk, yelled as his feet twisted. Natasha, Megan, and Miranda looked at me.

I matched David's movement and put a hand on his shoulder. He scooted again, lurching. His desk hit Miranda's desk, knocking her binder to the floor.

"Get out your *Fahrenheit 451* character-development notes," I told the class, exchanging David's yellow card for a red card.

After the bell, David stood by the door, adjusting the collar on his polo shirt. "You're on a short leash," I said, moving the desks that had shifted during the period back to their original spots.

"Bark."

I shouldn't have compared David to a dog, but his sly subversion and ironic detachment made me compassionless. David feels no joy or pride in doing meaningful work or contributing to the class. His obvious insecurities prevent students around him from learning. I took his red card and pointed toward the door.

Feb. 16

The prompt: *In* Fahrenheit 451, *Montag says, "We need to be really bothered once in a while. How long is it since you were really bothered? About something important, about something real?"*[5]

Here are some excerpts from students' journals:

EllaMay: *I have three things. When you're hungry but can't decide what you want to eat, so you end up not eating or you eat a whole bunch of things and then feel unsatisfied. Second, it really bugs me when people add a plural to a place*

---

[5] Ray Bradbury, *Fahrenheit 451* (New York: Simon & Schuster, 1950), 52.

like Fred Meyer. It's not Fred Meyer's. *Finally, the nail biting along with hair chewing. You don't know what you've touched or what those other things have touched, and then you put it in your mouth. And oh, a fourth. I may have qualities that put me into the classic high school cheerleader category, but when I feel it is called for and necessary, I will show the depth of my character.*

Celina: *Some people exaggerate so much it's unbearable, but you can't respond like, "No, that's impossible—you did not say her name a million times," because then that person would get all defensive and say s/he was exaggerating, which makes you look like this person who is so insecure with off-set data, that they have to make little snide remarks about someone's inaccurate estimate, and then everyone thinks you're impatient or high-strung. Why can't we, as a society, band together, and start sharing ideas and stories more realistically? No, there was not "like a trillion police outside the house"—that's way too much. In fact, that's just silly. There were probably around ten policemen give or take.*

Natasha: *Nowadays, because of the digital camera, people go trigger-happy producing thousands of images. In the old days of film, I bet there was an anticipation for the memory. Now people take a picture, and two seconds later, they look at themselves looking at the camera in the same spot they're currently standing in.*

Mason: *Like, okay, criticize me all you want. Critique me, humiliate me, make me redo my work, put me down, stomp on my childhood imagination, but when I do go through and make the corrections and suggestions you oh so non-hesitantly throw at me, and I approach you with a piece of work literally steaming with new brilliance, instead of just snatching it up and putting it down, LOOK AT IT! and then say something like, "Wow, Mason, this is some nice work you got here, way to go." I mean, is it really that difficult to tell me face to face? I want to watch your lips move and your eyes catch mine and hear your vocal cords vibrating and your tongue working.*

Pippa: *Yeah so there are lots of things, but I'm not going to name them because it would fill the whole page with peopel . . . yeah.*

> *Pippae*
>
> *ummm, i spelled people wronge in pen!!! Sorry*

UMMMMMMM, I TOTALLY SPELLED MY NAME WRONGE TOO!!! OH MY GOODNESS, WHAT'S WRONGE WITH ME??!

Farah: *Exhibit A: I'm talking to someone I just met (a guy), and he asks me if I play fast-pitch, and I reply "Yeah, I do," and he smirks and says, "Really? Fastpitch is so easy." I get mad and say, "What the heck is that supposed to mean?!?" He says, "Well, it's pretty obvious. Girl sports are not nearly as hard as guy sports." Since I have a little issue with anger management, I stomp on his foot.*

Megan: *E. O. Wilson sums it up well in his book called* The Creation *when he talks about how we should not care for the environment out of interest for our well-being, but for altruistic reasons. I believe people who are under the notion that the environment was formed to serve us should probably not grow up to be politicians or biologists or oil corporation executives. But I have a whole list of things that bother me (I will keep writing until I don't feel like it).*

1. *How Doritos smell like feet*
2. *Needless repetition (on the radio or in school)*
3. *Pine needles down the pants*
4. *Legs cooking under a laptop*
5. *Just for one day in my life, I would love it if everyone wore something they made*

When we finished journaling, we talked about the book.

First period

KATY. I looked at the copyright, and it says 1950. Does anyone think it's weird we're reading a book that was about the future and the future is now? Because right now what they're saying is scaring me.

MARC. I've already read the book, and for all of you who think it's lame, just wait. Since this is my second time reading it, I want to say this book has a way of making you look at yourself that makes you see the world in a new way.

ALEXIS. Maybe the author wanted to write a book of consequences to let the reader know this is what will happen if we don't think for ourselves.

MARC. What I meant to say was the book flips you around, so you end up seeing yourself.

Second period

ZACH. When it comes to the part about the green blurs in the cars, I always try to notice everything on the bus. Even when the bus is going fast, I look for blurs out the window and try to see what they are.

NATASHA. Last fall I took a walk at night where moonlight filled the freckles on my face. Everything was slow and brilliant, and I felt like Clarisse.

ELLAMAY. I zone out. On iTunes there is a visualizer you can watch, and it has a ton of random colors and different shapes. And every once in a while, the colors and shapes will switch. It's kind of like the lights on Windows Media Player. One time in Mr. Walker's class he put on some music while he was talking and the lights showed up behind him, and out of nowhere I said, "Oooooooohhhhh . . . pretty lights."

Fourth period

TINA. Like Anthony and Renee, I'm finding this book confusing and hard to read.

ANTONE. I don't understand why Montag wants to show his books to Mildred's friends. Books are banned, so he knows he's going to get in trouble.

TINA. Don't get me wrong. It's a good book. I just want to know what the author was thinking while he was writing it. Maybe we should watch the movie.

Fifth period

NO ONE. . . . could talk without yelling, so students worked in groups drawing pictures of high-tech machines from futuristic movies they've seen. Tomorrow they'll draw high-tech machines from the book.

Feb. 17

Principal Pike started the meeting by asking us to use pipe cleaners to make symbols representing the people at our tables. Then we watched *The Triangle of Involvement*, a short film in which a woman in a business suit walks down a hallway and describes how a group of dedicated professionals can, in four years, change a school's culture. "Committed, systematic, second-order change is not easy," the woman in the hallway said. "It starts with the Freshman Focus, with blocks of energetic teachers phoning freshman parents, planning orientation curriculum, monitoring behaviors in a five-step referral system, facilitating drug intervention, developing shared classroom rules, and offering one-on-one tutoring to students failing more than one class."

At the end of the film, Principal Pike stood by the rolling television cart with a checkered quilt wrapped around her waist. "I think this is a good idea," she said. "Who wants to spearhead the initiative?"

The teachers in back flipped through magazines. I didn't want to commit to anything publicly. I thought about Mr. McKinney roaming the halls and wondered where he would fit into this work. Alice folded her arms.

"Well, our students want their graduation caps, and it's our job to help them, so I'm not going to ask anymore. I'm requiring you to volunteer."

We sat there while Principal Pike went behind the library counter and made sign-up sheets. Alice said it was better than the time she had everyone try on different "career hats," with yellow construction helmets representing people who didn't go to college.

Principal Pike put the sheets on a table and told everyone to sign up before they left.

People headed for the door. I asked Alice if she wanted to do the classroom rules group. She said sure—most of it would get mothballed anyway.

Feb. 18

When Paton knocks on my door in the morning, I give him a place to write stories in his binder.

When Grant strokes his tiny goatee and stares into the distance, I tape a list of incomplete assignments to the inside of his planner.

David completes medium-sized assignments so long as they don't interfere with his sleeve rolling and collar popping. I call home about his apathy.

Mason skips class to compose national anthems for imaginary planets. I talk with him about it and write about it in my journal.

See also: Justin, Tristan, Jay, Antone, Anthony—to the soundtrack of Josh strumming his guitar outside my portable door.

According to Pan legend, the Lost Boys fell out of baby carriages when their nurses and nannies weren't looking. Unclaimed for seven days, the boys went to Neverland to live with Peter Pan, the boy who wouldn't grow up. There are no Lost Girls, Peter explains, because girls are too smart to explore the dangerous world outside carriages. They stare at clouds and contemplate girl things instead.

Farah, the motocross fan and fast-pitch player, sits with her binder in her lap, hair swishing in front of her like car-wash curtains. The Lost Boys climb over furniture and make their needs known. Farah looks down and contemplates . . . brake fluid? I don't know.

She's doing okay in class, but Jasmine, Celina, Sue, and Sarah are failing. I haven't talked with them because they smile and play well with others.

When she got to school today, Sue told me about a boy puking on the bus and how the bus wouldn't stop because they were so close to school. She borrowed a can of Axe body spray to neutralize the smell.

"Tsunami or Gravity?"

"Mr. Smith!"

I said I was proud she had considered the needs of the group, and that we needed to talk about her grade. She frowned like the boys do and said okay.

After school I walked down to the counseling office to inquire about Farah. The counselor said she looked into it and that Farah's dad is out of the picture.

Feb. 21

Flat tire. The woman at Les Schwab took my keys and gestured to the waiting area. After twenty minutes a guy in blue Carhartts called me over. "Looks like somebody doesn't like you," he said, and rolled three nails across the counter.

Feb. 23

I sat in a plastic chair outside Principal Pike's office wondering what she wanted to talk about. The lamps and Christmas lights? The newspaper? Alice came out of the office shaking her head. Principal Pike stood in the doorway and loosened a strap on her overalls. She nodded at me, and I walked over.

"I want to get straight to the point," she said, moving behind her desk. "I want to know why you're failing your students. I have it down here"—she slid a printout across her desk—"you're failing 40 percent of your freshmen?"

"Unfortunately," I said, reaching for the printout.

"Research shows freshman year success helps young people do better in all of high school," she said. "That's part of the Triangle of Involvement."

Maybe it was the overalls or the orange turtleneck or the way she swung her legs, but Principal Pike looked like a girl who had climbed into an oversized chair at an amusement park.

"I don't think my classes are unreasonably hard," I said. "Adam has a D and does his work during class. I pad the gradebook with participation grades."

"But you're failing your classes," she said, looking at her copy of the printout. "Failing across the board. It might sound harsh to say 'You're failing' when your students are the ones with failing grades, but they're your responsibility. You have the keys to your students' success. The keys say 'Do not duplicate,' but it's your job to replicate the keys anyway, for all of your students."

"Everybody needs a key," I agreed, thinking of the side door down the hallway, which Principal Pike kept locked on some days and unlocked on others.

"Every student needs a key because some of the doors to learning are locked from the inside. You've heard that. It's a quotation I value."

"So I should help my students open the doors to their learning themselves," I said.

"You could say that," Principal Pike chuckled, "but don't go stealing my metaphors. Remember, you're working with teenagers. They may not understand us. It's their job to respect the process and open doors for *you*."

"And they fail if they don't," I joked.

"No, no," she sighed. "I thought we were getting somewhere. There are real doors and metaphorical doors. Real doors are doors anyone can open. Metaphorical doors are doors with the prize of enlightenment behind them. This metaphor is a task we cannot fail because students failing themselves is not a part of the Triangle of Involvement."

I pushed my toes against the front of my Rockports as I scooted forward in my chair. "Aren't there lots of reasons why students fail? Aren't there lots of variables, some of which are outside of our control?"

"Variables aren't the same as standards, and standards are what we teach, so variables aren't one of the variables we count."

"Imagine," I said, "you have a new zip-up binder organized by subject, but you don't care about learning. Or that you care about learning but you hate your GPA-obsessed parents and are calculated enough to fail classes to hurt them. Imagine you have no binder and your backpack is at your feet, and your class handouts are mixed in with a mess of candy wrappers. Or that your friends fail classes, but you don't know why. Or that you fail classes and have your reasons, but you don't care to say."

"I think it comes down to engagement with content. You could try using interdisciplinary curricula, like when I taught science and got a rolling cart from the library and—"

DIIINNNNGGG. The bell interrupted us.

"Remember, students who fail in ninth grade perform poorly in subsequent years," she said.

I said thank you and left. On the walk back to my room, the hallway rocked beneath me. Principal Pike hasn't been to my class since she told me to remove paper from the walls. She hasn't observed or evaluated me. I opened the door to Mr. Beyer's room and started talking.

"'They're failing,' she said. 'I'm failing.' Duh. I go home at night kicking myself because I know I'm failing. Of course I can do better. Part of me wishes Heinemann or the College Board would provide me with human heads with android bodies programmed for typical high school student behaviors. That way I could practice giving lessons with fake students before endangering real ones."

Mr. Beyer took a bite of his peanut butter and jelly sandwich.

"I'm assuming your conversation with Principal Pike didn't go well?"

"I need more practice. I need a warehouse full of robots. 'They're failing because I'm failing.' I know all this. I just don't understand why she has to be so accusing. She hasn't watched me teach."

He wadded up his sandwich bag and threw it away. "You could pray for a lateral transfer in the next lemon dance, but you can't go crazy," he said. "You're new. The fine print says you have to teach ten years before falling victim to administrivia."

I stepped close to his desk, feeling like one of his students. "I can't wait that long."

"Let me show you something."

He rolled out a desk drawer and pulled out a collection of folders labeled Certifications, Observations, Evaluations, Substitute Information, Clock Hours, Professional Development, Retirement, and Benefits. "Some teachers keep a smile file for thank you notes and drawings," he said, "but I leave that stuff out where I can see it." He pointed to a tack board layered with doodles and pictures. "All the other stuff, the stuff that makes me feel crazy, goes in the drawer."

Feb. 23

Here we go a-WASL-ing. WASL stands for Washington Assessment of Student Learning, the test students take as part of the "standards-based education reform" mandated by the No Child Left Behind Act, or NCLB, or Nickel-bee.

Two faculty proctors staff each room. One proctor sits at a desk in the front while the other proctor circulates and looks for "irregularities and breaches in the testing environment." Students' backpacks line a side wall. If a cell phone goes off, a proctor calls a supervisor. Room assignments are random, so students don't know the proctors, and vice versa. I'm in a room with pictures of football players on the walls.

Today started with twenty minutes of instructions read verbatim from a booklet. Then I gave the prompt for the writing task: "If you could be any age, what age would you be and why?"

One girl blurted that she wanted to be ten or fifty-five so she could order from the children's or senior's menu at Denny's.

I wrote the starting and ending time on the whiteboard and sat at a desk in the back.

After another twenty minutes, I walked around with a handful of pencils. I noticed a boy using a blue pen. "Pens aren't allowed," I whispered.

"This is the writing test," he said.

"Pencil only," I said, looking at one of the football posters, the player's feet inches off the ground as he grasped for the ball.

"Well, you want these?" he asked, sliding pens in blue, red, green, and black across his desk.

"I'll trade you for a pencil."

Feb. 24

Micaela said she came up with a list of questions to ask people on the bus because the ride was long, and she got bored. Today at the end of class, she shared some of the questions she has asked so far and the answers she received.

Why do some people purposely disobey authority just to disobey authority?
Because authority would not let them boogie.

Why do people get sick?
Because they're done boogying. Because organs and organelles in the body don't always function properly, and people can't boogie anymore.

Why is there religion?
Because chicks dig guys with beards.

Why do people fall in love?
Because they're afraid to die alone.

Why do people die?
Because they never fell in love. Sometimes people fall in love because they have too much time on their hands.

Why were video games invented?
Adults needed money, and kids who were afraid of going outside needed something to do.

Why do trees grow against gravity?
They're rebellious.

Why dinosaurs?
Because human beings need to be reminded they're less awesome than dinosaurs.

What does WASL stand for?
Waste. A. Student's. Life.

Feb. 26

Stolen gas cap and another flat tire. I sent an all-school email asking if anyone else had suffered damage in the last few weeks. Weyn Rider: flat tire. Camille Connery: flat tire. Lorena Grayson: two nails in two tires. Val Webber: three flat tires in one week. Jenyce Portnoy: FUCK YOU keyed on the passenger side door.

I cross-referenced our class rosters and followed up via email. *I compared our schedules and found the names of students shared by those of us with vandalized property. Please let me know if you hear anything suspicious from Nick Cornell or Ross O'Connell.*

A few minutes later Principal Pike was in my room.

"Under no circumstances are you to put students' names out on emails to other staff members," she said. "You need to respect students' privacy. When you go on a manhunt you rile up teachers, and I have a situation on my hands."

"How do I avoid getting flat tires?"

"Park in a different spot. Make fewer enemies."

I saw myself slashing the tires on Principal Pike's Subaru, but before I could hear the hiss, the bell rang. My planning period was over. "What's up, Smith?" Antone said, walking in and seeing Principal Pike. "Pee-wee giving you a lecture?"

"Don't rile up the staff," Principal Pike said.

I told fourth period about my second flat tire. "This kind of thing makes me not like coming to school. When I walk down the hallway, I wonder, 'Is that him? Is that her? Is that the person who vandalized my car?'"

"We'll find out who it is, Smith," Antone said.

"Yeah, we'll beat 'em up," Taylor said. "They can't do that."

The other boys and Renee cheered. Part of me wanted to approve the idea. Matt suggested I make my Oldsmobile look like a student's car by "pimping it with decals."

"If he's gonna have a saucy whip, he has to decide 'sporty' or 'gangster,'" Tina added.

"I just want to get home at night," I said.

Antone nodded. "But piranhas swimming around an aquarium in the trunk would look badass, wouldn't it?"

Feb. 27

Here we go a-WASL-ing, Day 5. Principal Pike delivered granola bars and banana halves to our room in black garbage bags. After five mornings of high-stakes testing—the equivalent of ten hours of time for proctors to grade their own students' papers and plan their future lessons—I've read and evaluated every handout and exit slip. With the exception of the night that I drowned my students' journals, this is the first time this year I've been caught up on grading.

Three more days of testing.

I logged into a computer and looked at scores from prior WASLs. In reading and writing last year, our school was ten points above the state average. In math, we scored five points above the average. The percentage of students failing is still 30 percent, 40 percent, and 60 percent on reading, writing, and math, respectively, but that's better than half of the state.

I looked at older scores. For five years in a row, math scores have been lower than reading and writing scores.

How can the math scores in Washington state be lower than the reading and writing scores year after year?

Maybe . . .

(1) Washington students are worse at math because there's something in the water (but water doesn't abide by state lines, and Oregon seems to be fine . . . so no?);

(2) the math teachers in Washington State are bad teachers, and/or the math teachers in Washington State are good teachers but not as good as the English teachers;

(3) the math teachers are excellent but teaching different skills and standards; or

(4) the math test is harder than the other tests.

Looking at the news and op-ed articles surrounding the release of the scores, journalists weren't asking those questions.

I predict that in the next ten years or so, Americans will embrace national standards to solve the problem of certain portions of state tests being harder than certain other portions of state tests.

I predict that by 2030, Americans will embrace international standards as a way of solving the problem of some nations having harder tests than other nations. Google robots may or may not produce a comprehensive, globally aligned and culturally sensitive spreadsheet of benchmarks, including building blocks for a rigorous, worldly education.

By 2031, United Nations education delegates will develop a global test that matches Google's up-to-date spreadsheet of benchmarks. Creators of the test will agree that the test should show cultural sensitivity by adapting itself to the racial identities of test takers.

2032: Students seeking degrees from the UN will take the test for the first time and find themselves, in the fifty-fourth problem, magically clicking on products that match their ancestors' identities, all available for purchase.

In the testing room, the daily weighing of the underfed calves continues. "Thirteen minutes left," I say. A few minutes later Principal Pike comes around with a snack, maybe a box of prepackaged cheese and crackers, the kind with the red scoops for the cheese.

Silence Is like Music
but Anyone Can Sing the Song

March 1

My honors students banged rusty tin cans on their desks, demanding points. "Points! Points!" they yelled. "Give us points!"

"I'm out of points," I said.

"You said points! You said ten!"

"The point factory is closed," I said. "We scoured the hillsides and mines but couldn't come up with enough raw material."

"You have points!"

"I have a few from 1998."

"We want them!"

"They're dull."

"POINTS! POINTS!"

"Listen. A teaspoon is a teaspoon and a cup is a cup, but if Mr. Foster gives three hundred points each semester and I only give two hundr—"

"POINTS! POINTS!" they yelled, pounding on the desks.

I awoke at my desk with a headache. Hole-punched confetti and tooth-imprinted pencils on the carpet told me Murray hadn't yet come through to clean the room. For some reason that was my worry: Murray catching me sleeping.

I drove home. Now I'm awake and can't shake the dream. Points are uniform, weighed, and portioned. That's what students believe. Teachers reinforce this belief because letting students in on the subjectivity and irrational rationing of points would undo some of their power.

March 2

I think Principal Pike observed me. She walked into my class during fifth period, fist bumped Adam, and sat in the outer circle of desks. Ever since fifth period rocked back and forth in their chairs like an ocean swell, I've been afraid they might at some point work together again, staging a coup d'état like students in music videos for Pink Floyd's "Another Brick in the Wall" or Nirvana's "Smells Like Teen Spirit," overturning tables and rebelling against the Thought Factory.

Students might one day work together like they do in *High School Musical,* singing and dancing "We're All in This Together" while teachers and lunch monitors clap along, but today I'm grateful that they stayed in their seats.

After about five minutes, Grant leaned over to Principal Pike. "What's up, Pee-wee?"

Principal Pike closed her planner, walked over to me, and touched my elbow. "Your students don't seem engaged," she said, and then left.

"Marshmallow be scopin' you!" Grant yelled.

"Did you have to?" I asked.

"She was at my desk."

"Upsetting the order is your job alone?"

"Yeah."

March 3

When students ask, "What are we doing today?" I respond, "Baptizing elves" or "Fighting wildebeests."

Back in September, I wrote the agenda on the board every day before class, and students walked in, scanned it, and complained. When I stopped writing the agenda, they asked why I had stopped. I said I didn't think students needed to premeditate their emotions from a couple of key words. Still, they asked, "What are we doing today?"

"Writing," I finally told Antone.

Antone said he did better with hands-on activities.

"Drawing then," I said.

"But English class isn't art class," Matt said. "Drawing shouldn't be required."

"We're writing about art," I said.

"I'm a kinesthetic learner," Taylor said. "I do better when I'm moving."

I put my hands on my cheeks and stretched my mouth into an oval. I stood there like that, as if in a painting.

What are we doing today?

Something strange looms on the horizon. Best to prepare for everything.

March 4

"When do we get out of here?" students used to ask, sneaking glances at their phones, counting the minutes. "How much longer do we have?" they would ask, unable to read the analog clock and unwilling to do the math after looking at the schedule and checking their phones.

Almost always, they found a way to waste the final three or seven minutes by packing their bags and comparing my class to someplace more fun, like the parking lot. They talked about which upperclassmen went off campus for lunch and who might give them rides. Then I taped construction paper over the clock and explained that an education is not a prison sentence and that I would no longer answer questions about the time.

Mason pointed out that I seem to care about the time when it comes to silent reading.

At the same time, Justin continues to work toward his long-term goal right up until the bell, scratching holes in his desk and coloring them black. I think he's digging tunnels.

"What did we do yesterday?" Andrea asked this morning. She stood by the door holding a note excusing her absence. "Did I miss anything?"

Paton was hanging out before the bell, writing on the whiteboard. *Silence is like music but anyone can sing the song.*

"Lots!" I said. "Do you know about the make-up book?" I showed her the binder where I write each day's activities. "If you're ever gone," I said, "this is where you can find out what you missed."

"But it won't tell you about the installation of the retractable dome roof," Paton said, turning around, whiteboard marker in hand. "I'll tell you what you missed. The ceiling parted. Chairs rose beneath us in stadium-like formation. We took turns standing in the middle of the room and explaining our childhood scars and saying what we believe about life."

"Don't go hypoglypsycho," Andrea said.

"Everything we did yesterday," I said, flipping toward the back of the binder, "is right here. This page will tell you about the assignments we did and where to go for handouts."

"Whiteboard hangman, heads up seven up . . . we played all the old games," Paton said.

Dear Principal Pike,

After you left my fifth-period class a few days ago, I thought about what you said about my students not seeming engaged. While it's true that a few students were staring out the windows and not really doing what they should have been doing, I'd be lying if I said I wasn't grateful for the momentary calm. A small group of volunteers had successfully shooed a bee out of the light fixtures a few minutes before, and Jamie, standing on one of the desks, had suggested we write dangling modifiers and hang them from the ceiling. She volunteered to help everyone in class brainstorm a different phrase. The class loved this idea, and since fifth period and I synchronize like this once in a full blood moon, energy was high. The daydreaming you walked in on was a counterpoint before we moved on to expanding an advertisement analysis students wrote back in December. I knew they would have questions about going back to an old assignment.

At the risk of oversharing, I don't worry about students in my classes getting lost in dreamy reveries. I think mental breaks in which we expand or clarify our thoughts can be productive—with certain exceptions, of course. If I look in Justin's eyes and I see the reflection of the tennis courts or the parking lot, I know he might be close to walking out of class. That's my cue to find out if he ate anything other than maple bars for lunch.

Anyway, enough with the excuses. Here are two ways I plan to do better when it comes to engaging my fifth-period students:

(1) Computers. I've been listening to teachers talk in the copy room. Apparently, there is a south campus room with headphones, speakers, screens, and Wi-Fi, and if I reserve time slots far enough ahead of time, I can bring my whole class. Students can sit at machines, click on boxes that make other boxes open, and learn about the world by staring through windows, perhaps with vacant expressions on their faces.

(2) Rings. I'm thinking about pairing up the boy in first period who makes lists of alliterative lies—A hurricane howls every time I sneeze snot or even sniffle, he wrote—with the girl who says her teeth are the ivory keys of Beethoven's legless piano. I'm also thinking about pairing up the wide receiver who makes his eye sockets burp with the girl who says her parents keep a carbine rifle under their bed at home. Can you see it? Can you see these young people agreeing to get married?

Before long, everyone will be engaged.

Maybe even me.

Derek

March 9

While David spit shined his shoes, the class discussed examples of dystopian society in *Fahrenheit 451*. The white seashells in the characters' ears are like headphones, and the bombastic programs playing across the width of their apartment walls are like widescreen televisions.

"Mildred's going to end up getting 'the fourth wall,'" Cameron said.

"Why do you think Mildred wants the fourth wall?" I asked. "Would it be worth it? She can't see a screen if it's behind her, can she? Would the fourth wall be a waste of money?"

"Maybe she wants surround sound," Cameron said.

"Do you think a fourth wall would make Mildred happy?"

"She'll probably start saving for the next screen after that," Cameron said. "If she got a screen on the ceiling, her apartment would be like an IMAX."

David unsnapped the leather cuff on his wrist and flattened it on his desk.

"She could get speakers in the floor too," Zach said.

"Anyone else?" I asked.

"The fourth wall is a metaphor for Mildred's entrapment," Megan said. "Mildred can have screens surrounding her, but if every wall is a television, and we rule out the possibility of trap doors in the floor and ceiling, that leaves no way for her to enter or leave her apartment. There's no actual door for her to escape."

David put the cuff back on his wrist and snapped it shut.

March 10

I was on my way to the workroom to photocopy a poem and saw Paton holding the sides of the soda machine with both hands and pounding the illuminated display with his hips. "Oh, Kaleb's mom," he said. "So good."

"Fuck you," a boy behind him said. "I'll put my shit in a jar and smear it on you, ICP-style."

Paton humped the machine more. "Oh, feels so good," he squeaked. "More, more." The machine rattled.

"Your dick fits in a quarter slot," Kaleb said.

"More, Paton. I love your cock when Kaleb's gone," Paton warbled.

"Paton!" I yelled from across the cafeteria. "How's your novel coming along? Is the main character getting in trouble?" He let go of the machine.

"I'm gonna dick-punch you," Kaleb said.

"Dare you to try," Paton said.

We had the Mr.-Smith-will-be-the-Voice-of-Reason conversation I'm getting used to: you know the rules, you're in a public building, etc. "I'm confident you can wrap this up on your own," I said. "Remember that in school you always have an audience."

"The audience said she loved it."

Kaleb grabbed Paton's crotch and squeezed. Paton howled at the lights.

I turned on the photocopier in the workroom. Paton is the kid who shows up early to work on his adventure fantasy novel in his binder and doodle aphorisms on the whiteboard. The day I tripped on a saxophone case sticking out in the aisle he used his feet to push his backpack out of the way so I wouldn't trip on something again.

I put the poem in the feeder tray. One hundred forty copies.

Think about your audience, I tell students.

I teach in Gig Harbor and puke from too many margaritas in Bellingham. In my Costa Rican loungewear, I'm all kinds of Vice. In my khaki and corduroy pants, I'm the Voice. I adapt to contexts like a chameleon. I want Paton to be more than a mouth for parents, ears for teachers, hands for employers, and eyes for himself and his friends' hot moms.

Help Paton be more than fragments and shades.
Help me be more than tectonic plates.

Twenty more copies.

Maybe when the development of the mind meets the transformation of the soul, and we care about cultivating our inner thinking as much as we think about who might be watching, we'll have something.

March 12

Pippa had a dream about my class and wrote it out. I read it over tonight's gelatinous microwavable meal.

I was sitting in class as innocent as possible while Mr. Smith was teaching his average everyday lesson then all of the sudden my spider senses start tingling! What was I to do? My senses told me my dad was in trouble, so I got out my phone and tried to call him while Mr. Smith was teaching . . . the worst idea ever. Mr. Smith stops the class and goes over to his desk and out of nowhere pulls out a huge sledgehammer. I'm sitting here on my phone wondering what is going on? As he comes over and swiftly grabs the phone out of my hands . . . I sit there in shock, wondering if I did something wrong. He puts the phone down and SMASHES it with all his might, his smile showing through his satisfied expression. Then he turns to me and says, "That's your first warning."

March 13

I stood next to my workroom mailbox holding a supply catalog, a copy of Principal Pike's typo-riddled community newsletter, and a spreadsheet called the Employability Grid with a few paragraphs about the lesson Principal Pike observed. According to the first page of the Grid, I am not proficient or distinguished in any category, and in three categories—Viable Assessment Methods, Organized Progression of Learning Activities, and Knowledge of Developmental Characteristics of Age Group—I am unsatisfactory.

Leaning against a counter lined with stacks of military-themed desk calendars, I turned the page and read the description. I could only get to the second sentence—"This classroom is a place of distraction"—before my hands started trembling. A science teacher pulled a toner cartridge out of the side of the copy machine. I tucked the paper in my pocket and walked down the hallway.

Principal Pike's door was closed. I joined a girl with a necklace made out of Froot Loops in the line of chairs outside the door. "Are you waiting for Principal Pike?"

"Pee-wee? Sure," she said.

"Why are you here?"

"Mr. Sanders doesn't like my attitude. I brought an apple to class, and when he asked if I was going to eat it, I said, 'No, I'm going to smoke it because eating isn't allowed,' and he told me to change my attitude, and I said my attitude changes every day, and he told me to go to the office. I don't care. Pee-wee can call my parents."

Principal Pike opened the door with a quilt tucked around her waist. Black nylons covered her otherwise shoeless feet.

"What do you need?" she asked.

"I don't want to go back to class," the girl said.

"Stay here," she said. "And you?"

"I guess I'd like an explanation."

"Okay," she sighed.

I walked in, and she pointed to a gray chair. "I don't want to take too much of your time," I said. Principal Pike walked to her desk. I looked at her bookshelf. *Seven Secrets of the Savvy School Leader, The Seat of the Soul, The First Days of School.*

"What do you want to talk about?" she asked.

"Since we never had our post-observation conference, I never got to tell you how much I appreciate you observing me. And I guess I was wondering why you didn't write more on my evaluation."

"I spent most of my time in your room looking around. Whenever I visit a class, I imagine myself as a new student. I try to be as observant as an owl. The learning environment in your room is colorful."

"My students aren't new," I said, picturing Principal Pike's head rotating two hundred seventy degrees. "We've been together for over six months. Most of the work on the walls is theirs."

"But," she said, "they do not have their graduation caps. The way it is now, your room is overstimulating. There is so much color and paper everywhere. It's distracting. I do not see how learning happens."

"Do you remember when your mom put paintings on the refrigerator at home?" I asked. "That's the environment I want, but with less watercolor and more words. I want to honor students' work by displaying it." I looked at the Navajo blanket above her bookshelf. "Like the way you honor the creator of that textile."

"Where did you find the paint? The ASB room?"

"No, no. The paint is a metaphor. When I display students' work, it's like a child's painting on a fridge. The students know I care." I reached into my pocket for my evaluation. "And if they're daydreaming or waiting for extra help, they can look around and revisit what we've done."

"Because the room is distracting."

"But on purpose. I'm distracting students from distracting their peers," I said. "Maybe we can agree on using lesser forms of distraction to distract from greater forms of distraction?"

"Staring at the wall isn't better than talking to one's peers," Principal Pike said, untucking her quilt.

"I know you probably need to supervise the halls," I said, "so I'll be quick. I'm not a perfect teacher. I know I need observation and feedback. But I'm not sure I agree with what you've written on my evaluation. I'm wondering if you could watch me teach an entire period."

"I think I did my best the first time," Principal Pike said. "I tried to stay balanced. Between you and me, other people in this building are less balanced than me. It's hard being liberal in a conservative community, but I make it work. I'll tell you what, if you can get teachers to stop sending me students for ridiculous reasons, I'll watch you teach again."

"That sounds great," I said. "I'd love for you to see more of the good things that happen in my room. You and I have spoken about the freshman failure rate, and we spoke briefly about the tires on my car and the newspaper, but those were negative interactions."

She rubbed a frayed corner of her quilt. "That's really what you want? Most teachers want me to leave as soon as possible."

"If you visited regularly your evaluations would mean more."

"The evaluations are what they are," she said, looking up. "I count on the day of the observation to be a cross-section of the year. I can visit again, but the evaluation won't change."

"What if I don't think it's—"

"Show it to me," she said. I slid it across the desk. "What were you doing that day? What was the lesson?"

"We were expanding two ways of looking at an advertisement to three or four ways of looking at an advertisement."

"What was the objective?"

"Analyzing visual text."

"Was it written on the whiteboard?"

"We talked about what we were learning before the lesson started, and students had a general goal of analyzing an ad from different perspectives. But no, I didn't write it on the whiteboard because I didn't have one objective for all students."

"Fruit faces the sun at different angles."

"I think . . . exactly. But I don't think I can sign an evaluation that fails to show what I do on a regular basis to help my students grow."

"You still need a focal point," she said, "and you can't abandon focus just because one tree is ready to be harvested. That's what happened when you let Adam ask so many questions about the time. Fruit metaphors can be tricky. Sometimes fruit hangs in the shadows. Sometimes it hangs in the light."

"That's true, and I guess my job is to help students blossom, fertilizing the soil with the mulch of their education."

"Oh, I think our school has had plenty of students fertilized this year," Principal Pike said, pushing back on the edge of her desk.

"Are we getting off track?"

"Maybe that's why your students are failing," she said. "You're off track. I'm off track. Everyone's off track." She pulled the quilt out from under her legs. "Learning needs to happen in the zone of proximal development, the ZPD. Lessons can't be too hard or too easy. Students can't be underchallenged or overchallenged. If students don't meet goals in the ZPD, we re-teach them."

The bell rang. I knew students were gathering outside of my room. I pointed at the door. "Thank you for your time," I said.

"Oh no," she said. "To be continued!"

Stepping into the Hallway

What happened is this: Principal Pike called me an unsatisfactory teacher, and I called Principal Pike a bad administrator. Principal Pike kept her version of events in her planner, and I kept my version of events in a sprawling Word document I thought of as a journal. If you sat next to me at lunch today, I told you I would have accepted a bad evaluation if the evaluation had been more thorough. I may have said a few words about being good at "accepting constructive criticism when it comes from reliable sources."

I arrive at school at five in the morning. I stay until seven at night. If the hours aren't paying off, I don't want to know. Occasional positive feedback would be nice, but if Principal Pike can't do that, can she at least stay quiet? Her evaluation is about as useful to me as a box of left-handed scissors.

I drove to Target after work and the air smelled like dryer sheets and everything was better.

I ordered a mocha at the in-store Starbucks. The woman in yoga pants in line behind me looked like a Target ad herself, like her hair was windswept because she had been flying through clouds on a Dyson vacuum cleaner with other Norwegian witches. She ordered a nonfat caramel macchiato and scolded the barista for misspelling her name on the outside of the cup.

After my drink was prepared, the barista placed it on the bar. The name "Derrick" was scrawled in Sharpie. I said thank you and tipped an extra dollar in spite of Lysa.

I made my way toward Supplies. Just past the twenty-four-pack cubes of Coke, I found spiral notebooks, tape, scissors, and file folders patterned with neon fish. I wondered if I might live in my underground mother-in-law apartment forever, if I might grow old and die with stacks of ungraded essays in my lap, a dried-out fish tank in the corner, and a garbage can full of Michelina trays. I shook the thought by looking for red, blue, silver, green, and gold stars.

I rolled through Toiletries and picked up eight boxes of tissue and a few other things.

A few aisles over, I came upon a plastic curtain, pearlescent and illuminated by freezer lights. A sign advertised coming attractions: P.F. Chang's entrees, TGI Fridays appetizers, fresh fruit, and Market Pantry snacks. I saw the curtain running through the middle of the store as a slash through the landscape, a wrinkle in time, a temple veil.

I rolled my cart to Music and Electronics where JC Chasez's album *Schizophrenic* was on sale. One of his videos played across multiple televisions. As two women seduced JC in bed, I thought about Justin Laroque's career goals. One day Justin might get his hot tub full of bitches.

Around the corner, I saw a brunette woman in platform shoes pull a crimson KitchenAid mixer from a shelf. Behind her, a small girl in pink slippers sipped a Frappuccino through a green straw. One day she might be addicted like me, I thought, as I put a twelve-cup programmable coffee maker in my cart.

In Home Decor, I looked at photo frames filled with black-and-white stock photos of couples, kids, and landscapes. "You swallowed a gray sun," I said to a girl with overcast hair.

In the Men's section, I picked up Merona flat-front slacks and a Mossimo dress shirt. I looked at sports briefs, low-rise boxers, and comfort flex boxer briefs. The comfort flex boxer briefs were longer and shinier than the sports briefs.

I headed to the dressing room to try on the slacks and shirt. Unable to see my profile in the mirror, I opened the dressing room door and stepped into the hallway.

When I left the dressing room and rolled toward checkout, I found myself thinking about the right-angled path around the edge of the store. Most of the racks inside the store are circular. Students in my class sit in two open-ended semicircles, facing each other and facing the front of the room, linear and circular simultaneously.

A cashier motioned me forward. As I put my items—star stickers, boxes of tissue, eye drops, NyQuil, coffee maker, boxers, pants, shirt, and JC's *Schizophrenic*—on the conveyor belt, the cashier scanned them. I entered my pin and looked at the sign above the photo station: *Take charge of education. Reward your school.*

I took the white bags printed with rows of red circles and ambled through the breezy automatic doors. Cherry blossoms fluttered through the air. It was spring.

Fifteen Years Later

Know what the two best things about teaching are?

July and August.

That's how the joke goes, and there's a big heap of truth to it. Some of my colleagues look forward to summer more than their students do. They start their Days Until Summer Vacation whiteboard countdowns in April. In May, they physically separate themselves from students, ducking into teacher forts constructed from filing cabinets and bookshelves while students work on high-stakes projects. The last week of school is a film festival. These teachers are not most teachers, but if I'm honest, I know how they feel because I remember the year I started feeling like one.

It was my sixth year at Renton, and the transformation was fairly simple and fast. One day the voice inside my head sounded like a July-and-August teacher. At first, I didn't recognize the discontented inner thinking as my inner voice because that's not who I have aspired to be as an educator. I loved my colleagues and respected my administrators. I cherished my students. So why would I be looking forward to summer break in March? Maybe some combination of professional restlessness, chronic fatigue, and daily overstimulation? Whatever it was, I knew I needed to monitor it closely.

A lot was going well for me. I was thirty-four. I had taught six years at Peninsula and six years at Renton. After twelve years of teaching, I was no longer self-soothing under my breath, saying, "Okay, okay, okay." When the usual snoopervisors and walking clipboards from the district office slid into my room, crouched next to students, and asked them about the day's objective, I no longer fretted. I nodded and continued doing what I had been doing all along before the rigmarole box-checking had begun. Working with my students was more important than putting on a show for visitors.

When scattershot scenes from lessons that had failed in the past flashed before my eyes or familiar laments about the devolution of literacy curled in my throat, I reminded myself I didn't need to share every dark thought or be 100 percent honest with my students. The feelings had surfaced, but they would go away. I could push through any given day's ups and downs with an even-keeled temperament. When the specific glitches and hitches of a messy twenty-minute interval eroded my patience, I reminded myself that the freedom to detach from moments like these was the reward of hard-earned experience. I could deal with most issues on autopilot because I had seen and worked through similar situations in the past.

By no means was I an exemplar of composure, however. Like most teachers, I didn't want to soothe the nerves of one more Preparation H parent—Preparation H being the process by which well-to-do parents prepare their children for Harvard. I didn't want to tell Solomon no, he's not a ninja; we can hear him eating chips. I didn't want to explain, once more, that "Keep your pimp hand strong" sounds like a cute goodbye but bolsters and aids in the normalization of violence against sex workers. But I did these things, and usually without being a jerk, because I knew articulating and upholding baseline standards of decorum was part of my job.

Yet this mechanized problem-solving wasn't why I became a teacher, and it wasn't the same as truly seeing the people in front of me. Driven by notions of productivity and a desire to protect my emotional equilibrium, I sent students away from me with strategies for solving their problems without first hearing their stories. Unwilling to sit with students and listen to the particulars of how Mom had insisted on a whole group study session for the citizenship exam or how a best friend had broken a brand new 3D printer trying to make beef tacos shaped like missiles or how Grandma wouldn't stop commenting on everyone's bodies at dinner, I stood in front of my classes and gave directions, an actor motivated more by expediency and self-preservation than by an intrinsic desire to be or do better.

I had learned this lesson—that details of my students' lives gesture toward a larger importance that I can see only if I'm paying attention—my first few years at Renton. I didn't understand why I needed to learn the same lesson again. I didn't see why I couldn't have thick skin without falling away from what I knew to be true. I had learned to leave school at a reasonable time. I had learned to save some energy for myself. These were necessary lessons. But how much conservation was enough? The toughness I had developed had helped me survive the peccadillos of teaching, but now it had become a barrier between my students and me.

Earl, I knew, would have thoughts about maintaining work-life balance while staying true to my students, about drawing the line between reasonable levels of workplace detachment and outright disinterest. Elaina and Janet would have opinions about staying consistently civil while doing away with unnecessary pretense. Their voices had been in my head for years. But when I sat down and tried asking them questions, when I called on my trinity of mentors for help, their voices were no longer there.

The year I realized teaching on autopilot was hindering rather than helping my work, I had the misfortune of attending several bad workshops and presentations. In the fall, I attended a district-wide back-to-school kickoff in which the superintendent said that summer is a good time for educators to do a little international travel and pursue their hobbies. A few summers ago, she added, she traveled to the Galápagos Islands to photograph iguanas. Another year she went to Borneo to photograph baboons. As an early thank-you for the good work we would do this fall, she had included her in-flight airline magazine–worthy wildlife photos in her slide deck for the morning's presentation. She went on to analyze the previous year's standardized test scores while Gloria Estefan crooned "Coming Out of the Dark" in the background and pictures of fuzzy dodo birds, squinty puffins, and sticky tree frogs rotated on the projection screen behind her.

Later that year, I attended a six-part seminar to renew my teaching certificate. The instructor spent most of his time clicking through PowerPoint presentations with overly eager peeling and checkerboard transitions. "I don't want this to be just me up here talking," he said on the first day. "Feel free to contribute."

We didn't. Every Saturday for six Saturdays in a row, we greeted him with the same stony silence my honors classes gave me on my first day of teaching fifteen years ago. At first, this was because the instructor talked like Ben Stein in his role as the economics teacher in *Ferris Bueller's Day Off*. A few hours into our class, the silence continued through a lesson about secondary vocational programs. "There are no summer jobs for American teens anymore," he said to our small group of educators, some of whom had students with parents who had worked on the low-wage agricultural labor circuit, "because the illegal immigrants stole them."

During the break, I overheard someone in the class lecture him about the impact of his comments. When he apologized, I thought maybe he would stop discriminating against groups to which he did not belong. He brought us back from the break and clicked to a slide titled "The 'Dos' and 'Do Nots' of ASB Funds." Explaining why it's important to keep accurate records for classroom fundraisers, he said, "Those ASB cashiers can be some hairy-chested broads."

He was as alternatingly boring and offensive throughout subsequent weeks, and I spent a lot of time watching the clock on the corner of my laptop. When he asked us to share how we model small-group discussions for students, I played a game that has helped me weather myriad terrible presentations, a coping mechanism that allays the dread of wasted time. Whenever a presenter uses the word *model*, I imagine my colleagues walking down the runway of a public educator fashion show.

Check out Ms. Deena, blessing us with a sneak peak of what is soon to be everyone's favorite Friday jumper! No denying it . . . the Rockin' Teacher patch pops against the denim vest. You go, Ms. Deena!

Next on the catwalk, Mr. Howe does it again with one of his famous graphic ties. Wait, he added a flash-drive lanyard! Functional.

Here comes Mrs. Cissero, looking equestrian chic in a Horses in the Mist fleece jacket. Don't blink, or you'll miss the embroidered appliqués that spell READ *along the sleeve. There she goes!*

The collection wouldn't be complete without Mrs. Heinen in black yoga pants and a Positive Vibes zip-up hoodie . . .

As one might expect, this man spent most of our last day of class infodumping every PowerPoint he had left. He worked his way through "incorporating student voice" and "aligning project-based learning with national standards" as fast as his honeycomb transitions would allow. I stifled a yawn. If Principal Pike is Exhibit A for the theory suggesting people get promoted until they reach positions of maximum incompetence, this guy is Exhibit B.

Rather than toughen me up in new ways or bring forth necessary tenderness, these seminars tipped me over, and my fantasy sequences weren't enough to stop my impatience from spilling into the class-room. In my English classes, requiring full paragraphs from students who spent their afternoons playing video games likes *Assassin's Creed* and *Final Fantasy* had always felt like psychic warfare. Promoting nov-els in a soundbite culture, as Barbara Kingsolver writes, "is like selling elephants from a gumball machine."[6] In my classroom, I usually countered this cultural distaste for reading with unabashed enthusiasm for the written word, sharing stories about the power of literature and excerpts from my favorite books. But when Arya stood in front of the class and said the white space on her half-completed poster project represented a "blizzard of confusion" for Chris McCandless in Jon Krakauer's *Into the Wild*, I had had enough. "Take your seat. Your laziness is brazen but boring."

In retrospect, I see how my baseline decorum suffered growing pains. I made snarky comments not only at breaking points but whenever the opportunity presented itself. Much of the talk on educators' blogs at the time was about teenagers being "digital native learners" and teachers being "digital immigrant educators." When it came to technology, teachers were supposed to get used to students showing them new shortcuts and skills. But when I walked into the journalism club after school one week and asked students to insert metadata into a Photoshop file, they acted as if they were pickling cucumbers. When I asked them to caption a photo, I swear they pretended to sew raccoon hats. I leveled with them. "We've practiced these skills repeatedly for weeks. Do you really need me to walk you through the process a fourth time?"

When I heard an announcement about one of my students on the speech and debate team qualifying for semifinals, I didn't pull the student aside and say congratulations. I went to the teacher lounge down the hall to share the news. "No wonder Dante made it to semifinals in spontaneous argument," I said. "I've given him space to argue with me all year."

The required evidence for a kidcussion was there. I wasn't seeing young people as people. I wasn't rooting for kids. I passed off pessimism as pragmatism. Familiarity felt like fatigue. Words coming out of my mouth sounded like the words of a July-and-August teacher.

---

[6] Barbara Kingsolver, *High Tide in Tucson: Essays from Now or Never* (London: Faber and Faber, 1996), 161.

Knowing I needed to nurture my own development, I made a decision. With moderate hopes of shaking up the dysfunction I was feeling, I sent an all-school email asking my colleagues if I could visit their classrooms.

A few days later, I started on the first floor in the choir room, where Ms. Dolan sat at a piano. In a black *I Heart Renton* T-shirt, glasses with aqua-green rims, and red cowboy boots, she was straight out of my fashion-show daydream. She paused a recording of a choir singing in Latin to address her class.

"What did the choir in this recording look like?" she asked.

"White," a girl in a velvet tracksuit said.

"How do you know?" Ms. Dolan asked.

"How they sound."

"If we worked hard, you could sound like that," Ms. Dolan said. "But I like the way you sound. You have a more assertive tone quality. I once had a judge tell me we should only do gospel music because that's what we do best. I think that's bull. I didn't say that to his face, but I did throw his score sheets away. How can you learn what your voice can do if you do only what your voice knows? What I'm saying is, I like the way you sound already, but we still need to work on sounding classical."

"'Gloria,'" she said to the class, and everyone stood. A girl in UGG boots set a thermos on the chair behind her. "Give me a round, classical sound," Ms. Dolan said. "Eli, hands out of your pockets."

"Glohhhhria in excelllll—"

"Sing like you're on *Glee*. Sing like you're a bunch of white children from California!"

"Glohhhhhhhh oh oh oh oh oh oh ohhhhh—"

I left on the long note and headed down the hall.

Entering the construction room, I saw retractable extension cords on yellow wheels that hung from crossbeams.

"How many of you know about the Lumberjox?" Mr. Carlson asked. "I've been plugging the hell out of it, so you should. This is the logo for our shirts." He pointed to the whiteboard. Two stick figures—one in pants carrying an axe, another in a skirt holding a saw—leaned on blocky letters: *LUMBERJOX.*

Blueprints for rocking horses curled on tables throughout the room. A sidebar on one blueprint listed parts: hindquarters, front legs, neck, head. The head included a nostril, eyes, and a collar.

I went to the video production class in room 104, one hall over. Antique cameras and viewfinders lined the shelves. Students sat at Mac computers. "This is Jason's autobiography project," Mrs. Jenkins said to the class, ponytail swinging as she turned to face the other side of the room. "Sterling? I want you to pay attention to the ups and downs in the audio."

Jason's voiceover started: "I live in Seattle but was raised in Fresno." The camera panned across a sepia picture of a Filipino boy on a trampoline in a sunny backyard, arms behind his head. The picture faded away and was followed by a video clip of a young man B-boying on stage. "I'm a self-taught dancer," Jason narrated. "I started by copying the Jabbawockeez, and now I perform at many places in Seattle."

Another day I toured the second and third floors. I had never noticed Ms. Sandoval's door covered in pi stickers. Peeking in, I saw her kneeling by a cluster of desks, her eyes level with a girl wearing feather earrings. "I'm going to leave you with it," Ms. Sandoval said. The girl took a sip of apple juice from a hockey puck–sized container with a foil lid. "I know this group of smart women can solve this problem. I'll be back in a minute to see how it's going."

I walked down to the leadership room. "What's impulse shopping?" Ms. Odam asked her class.

"You keep buying and buying," a girl with leopard-print slip-ons said, "and you don't ask, 'Do I really need this?' You buy whatever looks shiny in the moment."

"I watched an episode of *The Tyra Banks Show* about this exactly," a girl in a flower headband said. "People don't know how to control themselves."

A few doors down, Mr. Belfry's freshman health class worked on laptops. Students looked at pictures of food items accompanied by nutrition data. "Who would eat a cheeseburger without a bun, anyway?" a boy in an orange shirt yelled out.

"Pop-Tarts aren't coming up," another boy said.

"Some name brands won't show up," Mr. Belfry answered. "You have to enter 'fruit-filled toasted pastry.'"

Mr. Belfry motioned for me to come further inside. I took a seat by his desk, where wallet-sized homecoming and prom pictures covered the sides of his file cabinets.

"I thought you said you were healthy," the boy in the orange shirt said to the girl sitting next to him. "So what's with the meat pizza with thick crust followed by a chicken nugget Lunchable? It's called a *Lunch*able."

Mr. Belfry walked over. "Don't be hatin' cause you're jealous of her grains," he said, "or her honesty. This is about analyzing yourself."

"It's not all grains," the boy said.

"Your calories come from fat and sugar," the girl said.

"How might you both increase your fiber and proteins?" Mr. Belfry asked.

"Add Hawaiian pizza," someone across the room suggested. I stayed a few more minutes before going to Mr. Kaplan's eleventh-grade US history class on the third floor. In his room, the desks were arranged in a circle. Students sat behind paper nameplates representing groups of people.

A girl in a puffy jacket had the floor. "In the Declaration of Natural Rights, it says all men are created equal, and there's no distinction between rich and poor," she said, speaking on behalf of Poor White

Men, "so we think you should uphold our rights."

A boy in a black Adidas tank top spoke for Women. "We don't support this document. It says all men are created equal, but women are not included. We don't like that women can't vote or work outside the house unless men tell them to."

A girl twisting the plastic on a sleeve of crackers responded on behalf of Native Americans. "You didn't come here to help us. You came here to profit off of us. You think you're an undefeatable superpower, but there are other superpowers too. Spain, Portugal, France."

A boy in the Continental Congress stood up. "Not true," he said. "We didn't call it the Declaration of Profit. How does it make sense for us to profit if it's called a declaration of *independence*?"

"You're using the right words but avoiding any commitment to the right actions," said the girl with the crackers. "You people in ruffles are savages."

Our school was short on substitute teachers that year. A few weeks after my tour of the school, I gave up my planning period to fill in for a PE teacher with an injured back. The secretary warned me that students had already "gone through" two substitutes before me, knocking one substitute unconscious by throwing a basketball at her head and inspiring the other to quit by rolling sets of free weights at her. I stuck to the basics: basketball on one side of the gym, volleyball on the other.

In my second period class, a few students warned me against giving Tim Best a detention because he had Cloroxed Mrs. Heinen's coffee the year before.

I shrugged and said, "I guess we'll see what happens."

When less than a third of the students in that class, and somewhere around half of the students in my other classes, turned in their final essays, I worried more about the effort I would put into grading the stacks of exams than the lackluster efforts of my students. "I'll be able to grade the stacks in three or four hours instead of five or six," I thought.

Then, during the last week of school, Erica, the teacher who had inspired the *Dangerous Minds* party, announced at lunch she would be switching schools. Our department chair had always called Erica our "canary in the coal mine." As long as we heard Erica whistling in the hallways, levels of workplace toxicity were within reason.

I took my catastrophizing mind back to my room and graded the final essays. Why did I think Erica had stopped chirping? She hadn't. Erica loved Renton. She could be leaving for any number of reasons. I was reading the situation a certain way. Looking up from the fifth of seventy-one essays, I realized I didn't want to comment in the margins of students' work anymore. I didn't want to feel Schadenfreudeian relief at low turn-in rates for assignments. Maybe this paragraph in front of me, this chunk of text exploring two authors' opinions on the value of travel, would be the last paragraph of student work I would ever have to read.

For whatever reason, these scenes—the unconscious substitute on the gym floor, the canary in the coal mine, the ungraded stack of papers on the teacher's desk, the toxic cup of coffee steaming next to it—stuck with me. My tour of the building had helped me escape the world of my head, but I still wasn't sure if what I was suffering was a natural plot point in the arc of a regular teaching career, or what, exactly, was causing it. I couldn't help but feel like I needed to escape my school too.

FOURTH QUARTER

Live Your Life
More Yellow Instead of Grey

March 15

Found in the Question Jar and definitely from Mason:

> *This book I'm reading is as boring as spending a week in woodworking class making doorstops for teachers or writing lab reports in biology on fruit fly mutation. A good story needs unlikely love, screaming in the face of danger, Michael Bay sounds, sexy dirt, and impossible makeup.*
> *Wolf*

March 16

I had a dream David said I got into teaching for my ego.

I drank my morning coffee in the doorway of my apartment and thought about the dream. I spend five class periods every day reading students' faces for signs of my presence. Do you see me? Hear me?

I have something important to share, and I would like you to write it down.

When I'm teaching, I stand between the two tips of my horseshoe seating arrangement, in the middle of everyone. I do this because sometimes a group of thirty-three teenagers needs a front-of-the-room voice to clarify misunderstandings, redirect behavior, or make a point about the reading.

The best teachers don't need to stand in the front, I know, because their personalities contain staging powers of their own, platforms and risers that fold out of their bodies like Transformer appendages. I don't have those yet, so I stand in the front and make points by writing them on the whiteboard or overhead projector.

I have something important to share.

Good teachers should have specialized knowledge that supersedes the knowledge of their students. Good teachers should be charismatic in their delivery while remembering they are there to be of service. I'm young, but what I lack in experience I hope I make up for with what I know. Or what I think I know.

I walked into my apartment and dumped the remains of my coffee in the sink. I got a bowl of Mallow Oats.

I'm thinking about David commenting about my ego in my dream because I think I understand what's at stake. Education should help unhappy people in boring jobs pass the time in ways that unhappy people without an education cannot. But it must also do more than help people pass the time. Education that only prepares people for the world as it exists, that instructs them on how to best survive or rise to the top of oppressive business and political structures, is insufficient. Education should create new structures too.

That's multifaceted work, and it differs from day to day. One day I'm a sergeant marching through rows of recruits. Another day I'm a talk show host weaving through a studio audience. One day I'm a specialist. Another day I'm a generalist. The day after that, if David is to be believed, I'm the newest cast member on the latest medical drama.

"We can't play God!" a colleague screams at me in the operating room, scalpel in hand.

"We play God every day," I say in a gravelly voice.

I showered and washed my hair. Mom called and asked how work was going. Sitting on my futon wrapped in a towel, I told her about my conversation with Principal Pike and my dream about David commenting on my ego.

"You've always internalized things deeply," she said.

"This time it's your fault," I said. "You're the one who talked me into this job in the first place. Whenever I was considering my future, you made me feel like I wouldn't be marketable. 'What are you going to do when you graduate? What are you going to do for work?'"

"What would you have done with your creative writing degree?"

"Been more inspired."

"Inspiration isn't the same as work. Our work can of course inspire us, and we can bring inspiration into our places of work, but the two aren't the same."

"I could have a normal job."

"A normal job? You have one, and you should be grateful you got into it for the right reasons."

"To please my mom."

"To please your mom who wants you to be able to pay the rent."

I'm in a towel, a little bony. My skin is cool. Can I rest my chin on your shoulder, Idaho Girl, so my ear touches your cheek? I should warn you: I internalize things deeply.

March 20

"Mr. Smith started the poetry unit in the coolest way. There weren't any handouts. He played a bunch of music. Can you believe it? Mr. Smith likes Nas."

The idea was to play a song or two and pause for students to develop their notions of Nas being a modern-day Shakespeare.

"He asked if we liked rap music. Like, *duh*. Then he asked if we liked poetry. We looked around because we didn't know what he was talking about. And you know what? Mr. Smith said rap music *is* poetry."

That's not what happened.

What happened: I photocopied lyrics from Nas songs, projected the lyrics, and played clips from "If I Ruled the World," "Hero," and "Nostradamus." A few students nodded. "Are these songs poetry?" I asked.

"All songs are poetry," Marissa said, running her fingers through her hair.

"All songs?" I asked.

"All songs."

"Only good songs," Adam qualified, twisting his ball cap backward.

"Good is subjective," Marissa said. "That's the point. That's why we need to say everything is poetry or nothing is."

"I was wondering," Jamie said, crossing her arms over her jacket. "Is classical music poetry? Because classi—"

Adam and Marissa mouthed insults. "Adam, Marissa, stop talking," I said. Derrell rolled his pen across his desk. "Derrell, Jamie has the floor. Marissa, face me."

"Is classical music poetry?" Jamie continued. "Because without any words—"

"Nintendawg!" Grant yelled at Brian, who stood at the door with a note in his hand.

"Chicken Finga Tree Man," Adam said.

"Did you get a lot of frags?" Grant asked.

"Beat the whole thing," Brian said.

"You skipped class for a video game?" Jamie asked.

"Bragging rights. First-person sci-fi trilogy."

I told everyone to grab a poetry packet from the corner and start reading.

Far from the poetry unit launch I had in my mind, but what did I expect? When I write out the rest of the unit, I need to forget what I've seen in movies.

March 22

This afternoon in the workroom I saw Principal Pike crouching in a floral dress over a blue recycling bin. The pink paper in my mailbox was an invitation for a barbecue at her house. She stood next to the recycling bin, pulling out invitations teachers had tossed.

I couldn't stop thinking about it. After school, I hauled my kayak to the beach, stepped into the water, and pushed off. The clouds gathered around the mountain like the mountain was famous. My oar cut through the water as I paddled past houses in colors that matched the landscape: green, blue, pearl, sand.

I saw three herons with bobbing heads: Huey, Dewey, and Louie.

The bottom of my kayak scraped a cement pillar under the water. Looking ahead, I saw a row of pilings from an old dock. I paddled in a figure eight, cutting right and left, avoiding the pillars.

I balanced my oar across the top of the kayak and extended my gaze along the shore.

I recognized her posture. Principal Pike stood knee-deep in the water, fishing out neon pink invitations. The surface of the water was slick and spectral, and when she saw me, she held out a soggy white mess. "Is this yours?" she yelled. "It looks like a journal from one of your classes."

April 5

While writing a unit plan, I consider Abraham Maslow's hierarchy of needs and Howard Gardner's multiple intelligences. I try to remember that with every text I include, young people will get ideas about cultural literacy, accessibility, and the canon. I look at the spreadsheet of standards I'm supposed to teach and ask myself if I can push a few of the bricks through the wall so a little light will shine through. I look for opportunities for students to move around and talk, remembering I will need to be explicit about when to move, where to move, how to position chairs and arrange desks, how to pick and review roles, who to look at and talk to, and what to do if a group member only wants to talk about freezing grasshoppers in biohazard bags. I remind myself the unit has to be for everyone, even the fourth-period fire-cracker who thinks "You are special" means "You are exceptional" and "You are exceptional" means "You are the exception" and "You are the exception" means you can say what you want whenever you want to whomever you want. I assume deep down this firecracker is some-what beside himself with anticipation and glee at the prospect of over-coming his impulses.

Writing a unit is like planning a trip into the wilderness, plotting elevation gains and losses, picking the nights we'll navigate by head-lamp and the nights we'll navigate by stars. Bathroom breaks, bell schedules, the principal's presence, the president's laws, and com-puter lab availability mean nothing to me.

Romeo and Juliet makes up the bulk of our poetry unit, and I've planned it.

April 13

Dear Mr. Smith,

You gave us an extra credit assignment, a poem. The day you gave the class the assignment I was delighted and excited to do it so I got started right away. I had almost finished when I realized I didn't like it. So I tried again but the words weren't there. I believe in order to write a meaningful poem, for yourself or for others, the words have to come from your heart. You have to be in a state of mind where you enjoy the vulnerability of letting your protected feelings spill onto a piece of paper. I tried to write a good, heartfelt descriptive poem but the seven times I tried didn't seem right. I will continue trying to write this kind of poem until it is the way I want and I have conquered the barrier of my mind, even though it won't be extra credit anymore. Just thought you should know.

Thanks for the opportunity,
Natasha

Natasha,

I agree it can be satisfying to watch a poem grow. Sometimes that happens for me, and I'm ecstatic. But what do you think about other genres of writing? Does a person need to feel inspired to write short stories or essays? Do you think teachers should make students write when they aren't inspired?

Writing is art, and writing is science. An uninspired scientist can conduct an experiment in a laboratory even if he or she isn't "feeling it." It's nice to "grow" a poem with water and soil and sun, but sometimes writers don't have the luck of weather or the privilege of land and don't get to act like gardeners or farmers. We have to wash our hands in the laboratory and go about creating circumstances for growth. We set up control groups, contrive situations, and make models. We cross our fingers for good results.

You wrote, "I will continue trying to write this kind of poem until it is the way I want and I have conquered the barrier of my mind." I admire your diligence. Too bad your inspiration is fickle. (Not being sarcastic.) Let me know if you have any ideas about how to make inspiration more constant. I know a few people who struggle with that.

Mr. Smith

Dear Mr. Smith,

I totally understand where you are coming from. You like all types of writing, right? I am a different person.

You probably won't agree, but I don't think nonfiction and research are art. I think art comes from the heart and sometimes from the brain. And I think what is considered art can be different for different people. It all depends on what a person is passionate about.

For example, I love swimming and consider it an art. But doing the dishes or writing a twelve-page essay comparing the birthplace of grammar to the birthplace of spelling (don't get any ideas) might not be art because I would approach the subject in an unenthused and inartistic way. But if we made an interesting theatrical version of the comparison of the birthplaces of grammar and spelling and performed it in front of the class like a beautiful Shakespearean play, then . . .

I guess there are different ways of looking at things, and if you approach every-

thing in a positive way then everything might be considered art. And you would live your life more yellow instead of grey.

You'll see I have completed the poem. I suppose someone somewhere might think it's great, but that doesn't mean much to me yet.

Natasha

April 15

The imaginary trip into the wilderness comes back to me when I'm writing lessons. Some days if I'm feeling on my game, I close my eyes and see my students on a grassy knoll on top of a mountain, *Sound of Music*-style. I imagine they're a band of happy singers swinging brown satchels and candy-stripe suitcases in the open air. I'm Julie Andrews in this scenario, and my students are singing like the von Trapp children.

Most days, though, I close my eyes and see my students gathered together on a snowy, precipitous mountain ridge. I'm the trip leader on a lockstep march toward Mount Doom, the heart of the black land. Students' backpacks are stuffed with binders, allergy pills, shin guards, spiral notebooks, seashell headphones, antidepressants, plastic retainers in cases, waterproof volumizing mascara, Jergens ultra-healing lotion, and boxes of World's Finest Chocolate.

"Where are we going?" they want to know. "When does the activity bus pick us up? Why is the sky getting dark? Why is there so much uphill on this trip?"

"It's a mountain," I say.

"The mountain we're supposed to piss on?" Mason asks.

I hear their justified and unjustified opinions. I hear bits of gossip—Brian got the strobe light for his shower, and Mr. Beyer is the coolest. I ask Celina if this counts for the spelling walk she wanted to do. She says no and asks if there will be a castle along the way, if there will be a place for food and water. Pippa says she needs to clean her ear piercing. "There's going to be a castle soon," I say. "You can use the bathroom there."

"But I don't have a dungeon pass," she says.

"The guards will have one," I say.

Pippa stomps a foot. A rock tumbles from the ledge. As rocks collide and crash below us, she fiddles with the turquoise bead on her ear and swings her pink backpack to the side to remove a box of powdered donuts and a pepperoni stick.

"What class do you have next?" she asks Marissa.

"Mr. Walker," Marissa says.

I forget students are scheduled for several other adventures after our mountain expedition. I try to remember that they probably get lectured and advised on every single one of these trips. Points are important, one leader says. Points are not important, another leader counters. One leader trusts students until they mess up. Another leader insists students should earn their freedom. On one trip, the leader calls externally verifiable information "data." On another trip, the leader calls it "evidence." One leader says a teardrop-shaped tick mark is a prime symbol. Another leader says it functions as an apostrophe or a single quotation mark. This assignment is worth fifty-five points, literature explores great ideas, science is not a mystery, you are the future, study the past.

The trip leaders are not as organized as they should be, and many of us say things to students that human beings on a journey of great importance probably wouldn't say to each other, like this meets expectations, this does not meet expectations, or this exceeds expectations outlined in the rubric.

Sometimes I imagine we get to the castle and students discover a staircase. I run to the top ahead of everyone else because I know if I don't add steps at the rate my students climb, they'll catch up and see me there, trowel in hand, half-empty bag of cement at my feet. "I just added these last few steps," I'll say, pointing to a crumbling staircase that drops off into the sky.

April 17

I went to Target, skimmed *Rolling Stone* and *GQ*, and made my way to the music kiosk. *Music for a Dreaming Baby*. I got some Market Pantry granola bars and NyQuil. The cashier asked for my license at the checkout.

"I'm sorry," he said, looking at the computer screen. "I can't sell you this."

"Why?"

"The computer doesn't say, but maybe you've bought too much," he said, placing the NyQuil to the side and picking up the granola bars. "Would you like to continue with these?"

I said I could get what I needed at the gas station.

When I got home there was a letter from Idaho Girl in the mailbox. She teaches elementary school in Boise and lives in a room rented from an elderly couple. I called my mom to tell her, but she wanted to talk about how easy teachers have it. "You have Monday off?" she asked. "Seems like this poorly paid teacher should divide his pay by the number of days he works. Most teachers aren't worth half of what they're paid."

"Do I count the extra hour each morning and the three hours every afternoon?" I asked, removing the safety seal from the gas station NyQuil. "What about Saturdays and Sundays?"

"Compare the number of days you work to the number of days people in the private sector work. See how much you earn then."

April 18

I paddled out from the beach. In the distance on my left, Peninsula High looked like a building in a miniature model set. Cars racing across the Purdy Spit looked like Matchbox cars. I rowed past the concrete pilings and let the wind blow me into a cove. Three herons—the same herons as before, I wanted to believe—floated on driftwood.

"Three blind mice," I whispered. "How are you?"

Billy Goats Gruff. Men in a tub.

Wise men!

Stooges!

O life, liberty, and greasy-beaked musketeers, look at your dingy feathers and charcoal caps. Look at your spindly three-pronged claws and your question mark necks.

You are monochrome gray! How do you enjoy this day?

Does Mr. Smith have a problem?

He is a little pig.

Sex, drugs, and rock n' roll.

Mr. Smith's wish.

As if!

He doesn't go out.

Hawks, ostriches, and albatrosses. Food, clothing, and shelter. Beginning, intermediate, and advanced.

How many friends accompanied Frodo on his quest?

Me, myself, and I.

The Ball of Paper That Is
Any Unsolved, Overworked Problem

April 22

I've been making a big deal about David coming to class. When he walks in, I announce his arrival, dust off his chair with my shirtsleeves, and ask if he would like tea. Today I took his silence as a yes and improvised a cup with my coffee maker while the class silently read. He didn't take a sip until someone dared him.

"I have Adidas just like yours at home," I said.

"Great."

I left Megan in charge for the last twenty minutes of class and took David outside. I should have told the people in the main office I was leaving, but I knew they'd make a big deal about the class needing coverage. I also knew the class would be fine because Zach, the instigator of most of the class's problems, was absent.

I remembered what I said about Mr. McKinney earlier in the year: *The least a teacher should do is stay in his room during class.*

Or not.

David and I crossed the parking lot and tennis courts and walked through the gate, onto the rubber track.

"Take off your shoes."

David blew a curl out of his eyes.

"We're switching," I said. He sighed and surveyed the track to see if anyone was around. The PE classes were gone. Two girls with cat whiskers drawn on their cheeks squealed in the bleachers. "You slide into my loafers, and I'll squeeze into your Adidas."

"Whatever," he said, pulling off his shoes.

I slid on his white and black Adidas Seashells. He put on my brown suede shoes and bent over to position the cuffs of his jeans. It felt weird to see my shoes on someone else, in different clothes.

"Now, talk as if you are me, and I'll talk as if I'm you," I said. "It'll work, but we have to start."

"Whatever." He pushed his hair from his eyes.

"Really?" I asked, pre-pretending to be David.

"This is stupid."

"I know," I said, moving a few steps down the track. "So boring."

"Do you think I like it that way?" he asked.

"I know you're trying to teach me," I said, "but it's not like I'm going to enjoy every assignment. You always think you know what I'm going to like."

He paused. "I'm the teacher . . . so I don't have to answer your questions if I don't want to . . . right? I can change the subject?"

"Teachers are always doing that," I said.

We walked in silence for half a lap. I found a drawing of Principal Pike with gremlin ears wadded up on the turf—it was a good drawing. David and I wavered between the first and second lanes.

"So," he said, "why don't you participate more?"

"I do. I listen."

"But you don't contribute."

"Listening is how I contribute. I take away what I need," I said. "But maybe, hearing you mention it, listening isn't enough. Maybe I should do more. If all I do is listen, I'm sort of being selfish. Maybe I should think about the rest of the class and what the group might need. Maybe I can contribute something."

"Because if you don't contribute your share of the work," he said, "you won't get your points. And if you don't get your points, you can't get good grades. And if you don't get good grades, you won't go to college."

We finished the lap we were on. Half a mile. Blackberry vines and Scotch broom stems poked through the fence around the discus circle. The two girls ran down the bleachers, yelling.

"I know what you're trying to do," David said.

"What?"

"With the shoes, with acting like you're me. I get it. I bet everyone is stealing your supplies, by the way. I bet Cameron is trimming his eyelashes with your scissors as we speak."

"You don't have much confidence," I said.

"I would never say, 'You don't have much confidence,'" he said. "Corny." The outside intercom interrupted: "Boys Soccer versus Lakes at Harry Lang Stadium. Varsity at seven o'clock. Bus at four forty-five."

"You don't get it, do you?" he said. "There's nothing you can do. You can call my parents. You can make me tea and walk me around the track. It doesn't matter."

"You really feel no pleasure or passion?" I asked. "You don't want to leave your mark on anything? Do you remember that part in *Fahrenheit 451* where Ray Bradbury talks about leaving something behind? 'A child or a book or a painting or a garden'? We need to leave something behind, something our hands have touched. You don't believe that?"

David slid off my Rockports and kicked them in my direction. "You say this shit, but you don't believe it," he said, eyes squinting as he stood there in his socks. "And if I believe it, then I'm the one who looks stupid."

When we returned, the class was split. About half of the class was reading, and about half of the class was hanging out by the door, ready to go. "Where did you guys go?" Natasha asked.

"Out," I said.

"To the track," David said.

I walked across the room to ask Megan how everything had gone. Students put their chairs up on the desks. "He made me walk two and a half laps," David said. "It was stupid."

April 25

My college friend Jason visited for the weekend. The first thing he did after complimenting my bathroom-and-kitchen-in-one was wrap his legs around the pole that runs through the middle of my living room and say, "This thing hasn't seen any action, has it?"

We rode our bikes to the Floatation Device, a restaurant where a plastic chain divides the bar from the family dining area. We ordered mini-corndogs and a waitress in sequined jeans brought us an unorganized mound of meat in a basket lined with wax paper. Halfway through my third whiskey and Coke, I suggested going to church, and after another pitcher of Pabst, Jason and I made a plan. The waitress recommended a start-up church down the road that meets in a school cafeteria because they don't have enough money for their own building. Jason must have set the alarm on his phone under the influence because "ocean waves" crashed into us right at eight o'clock on Sunday morning.

The congregation was in the middle of a worship song as we walked in. The lyrics immediately reminded me of a five-paragraph essay.

Here I am to worship
Here I am to bow down
Here I am to say . . .
. . . sounded like . . .
I will give you three reasons
Here are three reasons
I provided three reasons why the river symbolizes . . .
The kingdom! The power! The glory forever!

After another worship song, the pastor gave a PowerPoint on the apocalypse. His sermon included a timeline with dates. As I stared at a metal cart full of empty salad dressing containers on a side wall, I began to take notes on the back of the program: *NEXT YEAR! Cancel description of house assignment. Do end-of-world snapshots instead. Pick ending—Biblical, environmental, nuclear, whatever . . . AFTERMATH OF THE CRASH.*

Then I sketched my own snapshot: *Some people went to the mountain. Other people went to the mall. Neighbors came over to visit. We stripped houses of anything useful, like candles and matches and wood. People who used to have artificial fireplaces stay at houses like mine now.*

Jason looked at me and pointed toward the door. I nodded. His aluminum chair scraped the tile as we got up to leave.

May 1

Email from Megan last night: "I changed my hair color for the third time this year . . . which you predicted. But hey, you're a pumpkin bread fan, right? My mom is making some, and it's too much for just us but not enough for the whole class. Can I drop off a few pieces tomorrow?"

We stood by my desk this morning, chatting and eating bread. She said she overheard a group of kids playing with fingerboards on the stairs say Mr. Smith is pretty alright.

May 2

Standing on the corrugated threshold to N-7, Justin did his customary backpack toss across the room. He wore his usual low-slung jeans, long white tee, hoodie, tilted ball cap, headphones, and glasses. In one hand he held a ramshackle Discman covered with crossbones stickers. On his way to his desk, he handed me a note. I opened it and read his large, messy handwriting: *Yor supose to talk to the nurse.*

Justin comes to class twice a week. Sometimes he grabs tape from my desk and fixes his Discman. Sometimes he puts his head down, and all I see is his blond hair curling around the edge of his hood. If I touch his elbows or pat his arms or back, a voice says, "Somebody 'round here gonna get popped," or "I be straight thuggin' and duckin,'" or "I'm punking this monkey." Sometimes he sits up and scribbles circles on his desk while his glasses slide down his nose.

"Talk to the nurse about what?" I asked.

"Did I invite you to my party?" he asked, walking to his chair.

"You gave me this note," I said.

"It's not an invitation."

"You can write me another note and explain more if you want to, Laroque," I said, pronouncing his last name *Luh-roke* because I'd rather have him awake and engaging with me than not engaging at all.

"Luh-*rock*," he said, putting his head on his desk, "and why y'up in my grill?"

"Do you want me to talk to the nurse?"

He stood up, grabbed his backpack, and walked toward the door. A wedge of sunlight cut through the room as he left. Class hadn't even started.

I visited Nurse Winkler after school.

"He's legally deaf. He uses a school-provided hearing aid," Nurse Winkler said, pulling a tan moon with tubes attached to it out of a drawer.

"He wears this at school?"

"He picks it up in the mornings and brings it back after the bell," she said. "He needs it for three classes."

"What happens in his other classes?"

"The rest of the day he's in special education and gets face-to-face tutoring. He's learning-disabled, health-impaired, and probably has a developmental disability. The full-meal deal. One-on-one instruction can be helpful because he can't hide."

"He wears a lot of layers," I said, trying to process why I hadn't been given this information earlier.

"He does. He's supposed to bring the equipment to his teachers, including you, but he usually leaves it here."

"What does he do at home?" I asked.

"We aren't sure," she said, pulling a black fanny pack off a shelf. "We know at school he has this, and you can help by wearing a microphone." She held out a clip-on mic attached to a battery pack. "You'll be able to adjust the volume on his hearing aid."

"He'll be able to hear me."

"Yes."

"If he turns off his music."

"Yes."

"And he should come to get this from you every day."

"Yes. Sometimes we let him take it home but he's not good about bringing it back."

I looked at a shelf stacked with blankets and gauze. This is why Justin walks like a gangster through the halls. This is why he throws his backpack across my classroom. This is why he sleeps. This is why he slurs. I thanked Nurse Winkler, gathered the microphone and battery pack, and left.

May 3

Units overlap, so even as I'm getting the ball rolling for *Romeo and Juliet* with a few poetry lessons, we're wrapping up *Fahrenheit 451*. For their final projects, some students brought in trifold poster boards covered with articles they had printed out from the Internet but failed to analyze on their own. Some students brought in essays with more diary content than exploration of dystopian themes. Some students submitted work via email and, in their attached Word documents, didn't bother to make the fonts on the paragraphs they copied and pasted from other sources match the font in the rest of the paper.

I know it's my fault for failing to see what students were up to earlier in the assignment, but I wanted the nature of the *Fahrenheit 451* assessments to match the book's contrarian themes, to be less dictatorial, to celebrate students' capacity to choose.

The free-choice projects definitely highlight students' capacity to choose. Each project represents one individual's decision to contribute to a collection of mediocre work.

I'm choosing to see their mediocrity as a kind of curiosity: Is the teacher still watching? Does the teacher expect us to remember what we learned in September? Is it always true that when we write about a book, we should quote from the book and say what we think about the quotation?

To be fair, Megan's project is excellent. *Faber is named after Faber–Castell, an art company that began with the production of pencils*, she writes, asserting that Faber is *the pencil of the story* and Montag is *the canvas upon which Faber writes*. She investigates the history of the name Clarisse, which she finds means *clear and bright*. She points out that Clarisse *brings up many concepts that have never crossed Montag's mind*.

In the lower right-hand corner of her poster I wrote, *You bring up many concepts that have never crossed my mind!*

May 10

With the rhododendron buds out my window making such a show, I pushed to end the *Fahrenheit 451* unit on a dignified note. The last-ditch assignment: honor Clarisse's death (or death-like disappearance) in the book by writing a eulogy about her life—or your own.

Megan and Natasha stayed after school to make a display called "After I Die, Say This," incorporating lines like, *Farah loved softball with a fiery passion—yes, that's right, "fiery," EllaMay spoke her mind when the time called for it and sometimes when the time didn't call for it*, and *Clarisse needed wind in her hair and ice crystals thawing in her boots*. We talked about

Megan's parents' divorce while they worked. Megan said she was typing a page a day on her typewriter. I complimented her on her eulogy, which shines.

Megan didn't get walks around the track like David did, but she was concerned with learning everything and got closer to doing so than anyone else I know. She loved good discussions that made her feel like she was decoding life. (Not that she would ever want to decode life.) She dreamed she could evaporate or simply one day not exist and everyone would think she was out of town for a week. That's who Megan was: the kind of woman who might be out of town for a week.

She insisted on delicately pulling apart the ball of paper that is any unsolved, overworked problem so she could see every possible option and then find the overlooked combination. She liked knots in trees and had planted her own forest by the age of thirty-five. That's also who Megan was: the kind of woman who plants forests. Animals-and-plants-only forests, to be precise. Megan didn't worry about being part of the forest because she was the one who had planted the seeds.

May 13

As part of the work he's doing to earn his administrative credentials, Mr. Beyer has to practice observing teachers. He asked if he could watch me teach and take notes, and I said yes.

At 10:11, Mr. Smith walks over to the light switch and turns it off. The class quiets down and sits in their seats. Mr. Smith says he hasn't needed to turn off the lights since September. Mr. Smith clarifies his expectations and asks the class if they have questions. No one raises a hand. The class appears calm after the discussion.

Questions: Do you think the bell ringing at 10:10 could be used as students' on-task indicator rather than the light switch? Is there an expectation for how students should get your attention? Hand? Eye contact with you, the teacher? Recommendation: Try asking "What questions do you have?" rather than "Any questions?" "What questions . . . ?" operates on assumed inquiry.

Mr. Smith collects student work. A few minutes later, Marissa puts a piece of paper on Mr. Smith's desk and asks if she'll get credit for her work. Mr. Smith does not answer. Marissa asks a second time if she'll get credit. Mr. Smith says they'll talk later. Two students have their heads on their desks. Mr. Smith reads a poem to the class. He calls on Marissa, who does not have her hand up. Soon after, Becca blurts out an answer. Mr. Smith responds, "Good!"

Questions: What can a teacher do to ensure all students are engaged while reading? Do you think some students zone out because they know they do not have to read the text themselves? When it comes to students who do not raise their hands, what behavior do you want to reinforce in your classroom? Or is it even a big deal?

Throughout the lesson, Mr. Smith uses the "look" to redirect students.

Near the end of the period, Brian baits Mr. Smith into an argument. At first Mr. Smith responds by ignoring it. But as Brian continues, Mr. Smith informs the class he's going to stop because "we cannot raise our hands." Students are instructed to tuck away their outlines. Some students continue to talk as they reach under their desks for their binders. Mr. Smith notices the noise level rising and turns off the lights. Marissa, on the other side of the room, asks a question without raising her hand or making eye contact with Mr. Smith.

Questions: How do teacher behaviors reinforce student behaviors? Was the class warned before you canceled the end of the lesson? Why do you think Marissa acts this way? What are the consequences?

Derek, you've got room for improvement when it comes to instruction, but we all have weaknesses. One day your transitions will be so smooth they'll be slippery. Students obviously know you have an agenda and sense your urgency. The important thing is you love your subject matter and you love your kids, and the kids know it.

I see students who can be real problems in other classes participate in here. You challenge students, you are unafraid to laugh with them, and you treat them as thinking human beings worthy of respect. Your enthusiasm for the subject matter and for students is contagious. You model elevated metacognition and help students become savvy, self-aware, and intentional learners. I was impressed by your energy and the students' self-control during the last period of the day. You are one of the teachers students will remember long after they've forgotten others— because of the commitment, pride, and integrity you bring to your work. These students are better people for having had your influence.

One more suggestion: Ask the question first and call on students second. That way all students will think they might be the one who has to (or gets to) answer. For example, you could say, "I want everyone to think of step four and tell your neighbor. I'm going to give you fifteen seconds, and then I'll call on someone. Everyone should have the answer by then." By involving more students in your checks for understanding, you will raise the level of concern.

Thanks again for letting me watch you teach!

Earl

May 18

I know from *The Odyssey* and *Fahrenheit 451* that students groan when I hand out books. It doesn't matter if the book is big or small or illustrated, students groan. They throw their necks back and inflate their cheeks. So before handing out *Romeo and Juliet*, our third book, I went to the English department book room and nabbed the copies with Claire Danes and Leonardo DiCaprio on the cover. Juliet's white blouse hangs off her shoulder. Romeo's hair is wet. I grabbed paperbacks with nothing but the title on a cream background too.

Having a cool book cover with a few backups is my first anti-groan strategy. My second anti-groan strategy addresses what I perceive to be a slowly developing culture of low expectations by establishing ground rules that anticipate and address students' comments about the book before they say them.

At the start of class, I drew the blinds, dimmed the lights, and stood by the projector. "You are not allowed to say, 'This is a bad book,'" I said, gesturing to copies of *Romeo and Juliet* on a table and to the words *BAD BOOK* projected behind me. "You may say, 'I do not like this book,' or 'I would rather read something else,' but you are not allowed to say 'This is a bad book' or that it's poorly written.

"This is because you do not have the authority to override years of consensus saying it's a good book. If you want to say it's a bad book, the first thing you have to do is read it, and other books too."

"Second," I said, removing the *BAD BOOK* transparency from the projector and replacing it with *SOMETHING ELSE*, "You may not read something else. 'Can we read something else?' No, this is the book we're reading."

I picked up a copy and held it so its glossy cover caught the light. The projector, I imagined, outlined my body. My students' eyes blinked above the spread of desks before me.

"Third," I said, changing the overhead to *TOO HARD*, "you are not allowed to complain about the book being difficult. 'This is too hard,' you say. Well, school is supposed to be hard. When you struggle, you should congratulate yourself for being in the right place. Grappling with new concepts and language is part of what we do in this class."

"And finally," I said, "Stop pretending you've never read a book. I understand when you get a book from a teacher, you must complain. If the book is old or big or the font is small, you must say the book is old and big and the font is small. You say, 'I hate this book. This is a bad book. I've never read a book,' and you cheer, and anyone who likes books must stay silent or violate the law of the land. The truth is, you've read books. Some of you love reading. Some of you are afraid if you read this book you will contemplate the ideas hidden inside the pages and think about your life."

By fifth period I got the response I wanted.

"I'm not afraid!" Adam yelled.

"Is that Leo?" Pippa asked.

"Interrupting!" I said, turning to Adam. "You *are* afraid. And yes," I said, turning back to Pippa, "it's Leo."

"Can we start reading?" Grant asked.

"We won't complain," Adam said, "and we won't be afraid."

Unlike other periods, in which students' heads bobbed like seals while I distributed copies of the play, students in fifth period grabbed the books out of my hands. They stroked the covers and fanned the pages. Pippa leaned back in her chair until her gold hoops sparkled in the projector light and made a big deal about kissing Leo. Farah, Jay, Grant, Brian, and a few others wanted the plain copies.

We started together with an introductory activity from *Shakespeare Set Free*, a book with an odd title—has the bard been imprisoned? In what, a cell of poorly taught poetry?—that I borrowed from Elaina. We got out of our chairs and stomped around, placing emphasis on the last word of each line in the prologue. I let my hands fly like a crosswalk mother's, slicing and cutting through the air. I think the lesson accomplished what it was supposed to accomplish: get students up and out of their seats, call their attention to the rhythm of the language, and help them conquer their inner Shakes-fear.

May 19

My apartment flooded last night. There was standing water every- where, soaking through the carpet, seeping through the bottoms of the milk crates I had been using for bookshelves.

Not a big deal, I told myself, spreading out my books on the coun- ter to dry. I heated a Hot Pocket in the microwave and walked to my futon, praying to Poseidon to keep the water below the level of my mattress while I slept.

I dreamed all of Gig Harbor was flooded, and I turned my futon into a raft with a bedsheet sail to get to school. I floated alongside the shore of Henderson Bay and picked up students who didn't want to miss out on the next lesson.

I've always been the kid who couldn't stay away. When I was in grade school and bored in the middle of the summer, I would ride my Huffy bike to Lake Spokane Elementary and hang out on the swings, alternately pumping my legs in the air and dragging my feet in the dirt. I'd sit under one of the goal posts on the soccer field and read. I remember mounting the balance beam and leaping into the sand, practicing my Olympic dismount. Some days I would pedal my bike in figure eights around the tetherball poles until I tired and stopped alongside a dark classroom to cup my hands against a window and stare inside. I pretended I was looking at an animal display or a habitat diorama at a museum, learning about natural history. Here, I saw desks pushed against a wall, clothespins hanging from string above a door, feathered grass along the bottom of a display board, a container of highlighters in one corner, stacks of shoeboxes in another, with one of the lids open to what appeared to be the sky.

I'm Done with My Training Wheels

May 21

I was standing in line for swirled cheese sticks in the cafeteria when I overheard Megan and David at one of the tables.

"You used to be popular," David said. "Now you're always reading."

"That's a gross simplification."

"It was a transition her fans did not expect," David said in a sports announcer's voice. "Years in the spotlight and then—"

"—she pulled salami off her sandwich and enjoyed the mayonnaise-covered bread anyway," Megan interrupted in the same voice, laying the discs of meat on the empty sandwich bag. "To the extent such mayonnaise bread could be enjoyed, anyway."

"Where'd you get your bracelet?"

The line moved up. I hoped Megan would take her lunch and her copy of *The Perks of Being a Wallflower* to another table.

"My dad helped me make it."

I heard Megan's eulogy voice in my head—*Megan Buske wore a spoon bracelet around her wrist. She dyed her hair on the first of every month*—and I thought about the ways she has impacted me as a teacher and as a person so far this year. Next year will be different. I'll have different students. Megan will be gone. *I could never say it while I was her teacher but—how do I explain? Megan listened. She internalized my words so deeply I questioned every aspect of every lesson I taught. I thought long and hard before writing a comment on anything she turned in. Things that were supposed to bother human beings bothered Megan, and things that weren't supposed to bother human beings didn't bother her. She would be happy to hear us say that, I think.*

May 22

I saw Justin and his mom on their way out of Albertsons as I was heading in. "I have Justin for fifth-period English," I said, extending my hand as Justin looked away. We were by the automatic door on the sidewalk, next to a display of apples and oranges.

"Nice to meet you," Justin's mom said. She turned to her son, gripped his jaw with her hand, looked him in the eyes, and said, "Stay with me."

We chatted for a few minutes. I learned that she volunteers with the food bank and that she's not sure how she feels about the new Burger King by the Chevron station, though it might be good for teenagers. Setting my shopping basket at my feet, I noticed a package of batteries in Justin's hand. "For the Discman?" I asked. "Justin sure loves his music."

"How's he been doing?" his mom asked. Justin had one foot on the mat by the automatic doors. Every time the door closed, it opened again.

"He's been gone a lot, almost all of April. Sometimes when he's in class he does okay, but sometimes he sleeps," I said.

She turned around, lifted Justin's chin with one hand, and slapped his face with the other hand. Justin didn't move or say anything. He stood there, still as the pyramids of fruit to his left and right.

"It won't be a problem anymore," she said and walked toward the parking lot. For a moment Justin looked like the wooden bear that was outside the roadside tent across the street from the school, upright and unable to blink. The automatic door opened and closed again.

Justin unfroze and ambled after his mother.

I would like to say I didn't mean to wake the giant, but I suppose in a way I did.

May 24

I checked their *Romeo and Juliet* annotations. One girl crossed out all the conjunctions at the starts of lines and wrote, *I can't believe this book was published!*

Religion is not for everyone, Josh wrote near a reference to God.

Love! Micaela wrote. *Just like Vince and me.*

Marissa: *What a paragraph! I didn't know things would get so violent.*

Farah penciled long lines in the gutter. *How can you stop yourself from being sad? Sometimes I get depressed when I don't want to be, but it happens anyway.* And: *Did you notice? I'm pretty sure R & J never say, "I love you."*

May 25

Dear future,

At first I thought my students were fragmented beyond repair, but that wasn't the case. Many of my students chose to keep their stabs at coherence private. Some of them hid their deepest beliefs beneath a facade of glued-together poses. They may have seemed broken at times, but I'm pretty sure they were protecting themselves from the bullshit.

And boy is there a lot of bullshit—Sodexho Marriott delivering low-grade taco meat to cafeterias, Houghton Mifflin delivering racist textbooks to district offices, family members saying "Ds get degrees," etc.

I'm hoping none of this makes sense to you because we did a good job and things are better now. I'm hoping your young people don't have to dive within themselves for inspiration or guard their wholeness as much as the young people I work with now.

Best,

Derek

May 26

Students were drawing pictures of Queen Mab, the wish-granting fairy who appears in Mercutio's kaleidoscopic monologue, when Micaela told Hope, Pam, and Jessy that Vince asked her to prom.

Everyone wanted details—"How did he ask you? Who's doing your make-up? How are you going to wear your hair?"—and I pointed out the relevance: "Ooh! Do you see? Here we have wish fulfillment in the text, and wish fulfillment for Micaela. Maybe our Queen—"

"He asked me in the senior parking lot by his truck, with a dozen roses," Micaela said, "and I'm getting the Princess Look at Riki's Spa."

Marc, on Micaela's right, looked at Jacob two desks over and made like he was riding a pony, one hand holding the reins and the other slapping its hindquarters. I asked him to stay after class.

May 27

Not every day of *Romeo and Juliet* is coloring pictures and stomping around chanting lines of poetry. Our priority right now is reading the play closely. We'll act out a few selected scenes soon, but I told my classes there will be no fights with wooden dowels until we've read the whole thing.

"I will find the stapler," I tell students. "Read."

"I will straighten the piles of paper," I say. "Read."

"Look at this note from the main office. Someone has a pass to get out of class. Guess we won't find out who it's for until we finish marking this scene. Read."

Justin regularly puts his head down and turns up his music, so we read to the soundtrack of tinny guitar solos and buzzy bass coming from his headphones.

I tried to help him today. "We're going to pass around this mic while we read out loud," I told the class, removing my clip-on microphone. "When you speak into this mic, Justin will be able to hear you."

Grant leaned into the mic and thanked Jesus. Then Adam grabbed it from him and blew into it.

Justin grabbed his ears and yelled, "Down!"

I took back the mic. Two seconds later Justin was slouching in his desk again. I looked up to see Adam out of his seat, lifting up the edge of Justin's hood. He pushed Justin's right headphone off. Justin didn't move. Then Adam put his fingers in his mouth and whistled.

Without lifting his head, Justin rammed his arm into Adam's leg. Adam bowled over. Grant screamed with laughter. When the screaming waned, Justin murmured, "Pest by nature, thug by blood."

Ten minutes later we were back where we started: near the beginning of the middle of the scene, with most students sitting upright in their chairs, a few propping their heads on their palms, and Justin looking asleep, though not.

"Luh-roke," I said into the microphone. "You feeling this?"

"Luh-*rock*'s kickin,'" he said, head on desk.

Outside the window, the last rhododendron buds cracked pink.

May 28

Teachers took their places for the assembly. A few teachers looked like they were trying to hold up the wall with their bodies, the way they pressed themselves against it. After the national anthem, candidates for ASB officer positions gave their election speeches behind a podium at the half-court mark. The microphone was hooked to a small speaker on the bottom of a rolling cart, so the audience got bits and pieces: "school involvement and leadership . . . trust me to represent you . . . cooperate with class officers . . . money for winter formal . . ." When the final candidate for president got up from his folding chair, he skipped the podium. He went straight to the bleachers and distributed four or five Chinese food boxes to students. He pulled out his phone and turned it toward the audience.

"Mice!" someone yelled.

The candidate filmed the squealing and screeching, the stomping and stampeding.

When the gym was nearly empty, he gave his phone to a friend and walked over to Principal Pike, turning himself in.

I trust you can turn this into a teachable moment, I thought.

Teachers were buzzing at lunch, saying, "Administrators need to review speeches ahead of time," and "Does the ASB advisor even do anything? The only time we see ASB officers is when they need us to chaperone dances."

Changing the subject, Elaina said she had a good time at Principal Pike's barbecue.

May 30

I was in school for seventeen years. I have no problem showing students the ins and outs of the game: extra credit, points, keeping a planner, looking attentive when you're not feeling attentive, etc.

But I wonder whether a wise adult would do better teaching my students the assigned literature. As a twenty-two-year-old, I know what parents and teachers have told me over the years. I know what I've learned from philosophers and fictional characters, but I don't have much life experience. I've never left North America. In college I lived with painters, pranksters, a bi-curious man, and a biochemistry major, and I learned, again, what I had discovered at sleepovers at friends' houses when I was growing up: everyone has a way of doing things even when they don't, especially when it comes to leaving dishes in the sink, loading the dishwasher, and managing small spaces. The best we can do is understand our methods and communicate our preferences.

Given that some of my toughest conversations in life have been about silverware, I'm not surprised I sometimes feel like I'm moving through my classroom without any feet, teaching transitions between contentless paragraphs. Part of me believes I can gather precipitation from the clouds around the mountain in my brain and water a forest of trees.

I'm *still* growing up, and my students deserve more than pastiche paradigms. Students deserve, in every class, a teacher who draws on a breadth of experience to elevate classroom discussions, a teacher who can engender a multidimensional understanding of the human condition.

In inspirational teaching movies, teachers get sick partway through the year because they take on second jobs, visit students' homes after the school day ends, and give up what time they have for lunch to grade papers and counsel students. They're almost always new to the profession and trying to do good.

I no longer know if these kinds of trying are enough, I think to myself as I look in my bathroom mirror at home, whispering "Okay, okay, okay . . ." under my breath.

June 1

Act 3, Scene 2: "O I have bought the mansion of a love / But not possessed it, and though I am sold / Not yet enjoyed. So tedious is this day / As is the night before some festival / To an impatient child that hath new robes / And may not wear them."[7]

I delivered the lines to first period and asked, "So what happened?" I wanted to try more advanced activities like editing and blocking scenes, counseling Juliet on her last drink, and analyzing Romeo's final words. We might even discuss the role of fate. "Anyone?" I asked. "Who can tell me what happened?"

Maybe the language was too subtle. I provided a spoiler: a few scenes later Romeo slides like a snake out of Juliet's bedroom.

Someone will give, I thought. They'll eventually break and have to say. I waited twenty seconds. Kevin raised his hand. "Romeo and

---

[7] William Shakespeare, *Romeo and Juliet* (New York: Bantam Doubleday Dell, 1996), 66.

Juliet spent the night together," he said.

"Correct," I said. "Thank you, Kevin."

In second period a fly knocked its head against the Plexiglas window. "I'm surprised," I said to the class. "I thought you would know."

"Oh my god, you guys," EllaMay blurted out. "They had sex. It's the morning after."

By fourth period I saw the situation I had created. By fifth period I had put it into words: I was forcing a communal realization of a moment perhaps best appreciated by students who cared enough to notice. But by then I had already asked the question and Justin had yanked his head off his desk, pushed back his hood and headphones, adjusted his hat, put a finger behind his left ear, and raised his hand. His thick glasses slid down his nose. Marissa, Pippa, Adam, Grant, Farah, Josh—everyone—looked at him.

"Luh-roke," I said, standing across the room.

"Luh-*rock*."

"You have something?"

"Romeo tapped that shit. He hit it and quit it." No one snorted or laughed. My forefinger marked my place in the play.

"Why?" I asked.

"Romeo is the shit," Justin said. "Fly player."

"You like Romeo?" I asked, folding the book and tucking it under my arm.

"Hell yeah."

"If you could pick anybody in the play to—"

"I already said. Ro-meee-oh."

"A backup."

"Marsupial then because he's Romeo's homie," Justin said. "That's why right there." He reached for his headphones, pulled up his hood, tightened the cords, and let his head fall to the desk. He reached inside the front pouch of his sweatshirt and turned on his music.

A kid from another part of campus opened the door on his way to the football field and yelled "WE'RE HAVING A FIRE DRILL."

"C'mon guys," I said. "Fire drill!"

"Can't the practice round count for this?" Becca asked, recalling the drill we had for possible future fire drills.

"That was the point of the practice round," I said. "To prepare us for this moment. This is the real thing."

"It's real?" she asked.

"It could be," I said.

"A real drill? A real fire? A real 'fake' drill? You didn't know about it?" Marissa asked. Josh laughed. The alarm blared in the distance.

"No, I didn't. I mean, I don't know."

"Fire drills are always fake," Becca said.

"I'm not leaving the room for imaginary flames," Pippa said, crossing her arms.

"Let's go," I said, gathering my attendance binder and my sign, a piece of cardstock reading N-7 mounted on a yardstick. As the door closed behind me, I heard Farah's voice. "C'mon guys! Let's stay an—"

I walked to the football field and stood on the twenty-yard line. I held my sign high in the air.

I watched other teachers complete their fire drill attendance forms. I watched student runners deliver the forms to a vice-principal standing in the bleachers. The other vice-principal directed lost and wandering students, bouncing on chain-link fences and texting on their phones, back toward their teachers. I stood on my line and held my sign. Five minutes later I saw Principal Pike and a fireman walk into my classroom.

A minute or so after that, Principal Pike and the fireman walked out of the door and across the north campus parking lot, my students trailing in a line behind them.

Principal Pike, the fireman, and my students walked through the gate and onto the field. My students stared at their feet.

"I believe these are yours," Principal Pike said.

"Yes," I said, as my students lined up behind me on the twenty-yard line.

"They're precious," she said.

I shook my head.

But then I saw. Probably fifteen of them had a copy of the play in their hands. A few of them had their thumbs in their books, holding their places. I looked at the sky and believed it was true.

June 4

When we finished reading *Romeo and Juliet*, students had time to work on their essays. I crouched next to Josh as he copied down a quotation from the play. "What color should quotations be?" I asked. He picked up his black pen. "Red, actually," I said, "but knowing the colors isn't as important as knowing the ingredients. I'm glad you're using evidence in your paper."

Turning around to check on the class, I saw Marissa and Grant facing each other at what appeared to be an improvised foosball table in the corner. They had propped up their binder for barriers, and Grant held a wad of rubber bands twisted into a ball.

"I need everyone in the room to focus," I said.

I waited for Marissa to put down the plastic ruler she was using as a foosball stick and for Grant to put down the ball. Marissa walked across the classroom, her paper in her hand. "I'm done with the assignment," she said.

"You're done?" I asked.

"Done with Helen Olson."

She handed me her essay. *Why Helen Olson Sucks* was written across the top in blue, red, green, and black ink.

The Helen Olson style is too repetitive. It goes like this: "There are many ways to describe Bob. For example, blah blah blah blah blah blah blah . . . As you can see there are many ways to describe Bob." According to Mr. Smith, words like "for example" and "this shows that" are "training wheels." This shows that training wheels are good to help writers when they're starting out, but REALITY CHECK MR. SMITH, writers eventually need to take off their training wheels. As you can see, I'm done with my training wheels and ready to move on.

Marissa touched the padlock charm on her necklace and looked at me. Farah leaned forward. The class's silence meant Marissa was speaking for other students too.

"You're done," I said. "I get that. But you undermine your argument by using the formula to disprove the formula."

"I'm showing you I know it," she said. "I'm tired of starting my sentences the same way every time. It might not sound like it's repeating itself over and over when it's being written, but that's because we take so frickin' long to write anything. When you write one sentence every ten minutes you forget what came before it, and the result is repetitive."

"But aren't you writing better?" I asked.

"Yeah. I slayed the dragon, and her name is Helen."

"So you're frustrated and ready to move up," I said. "I was bored in school too, usually because the work I was given was too easy." I turned to the class and made my way through the aisle. "Marissa wants to move up and leave the rest of you behind. She's right to do so, of course. Let the record show that on this day, the fourth of June, Marissa Matthews slayed the Olson dragon and moved up to the next level."

"There's another level?" Grant asked.

"Yeah," I said, "and the only way to get there is to slay the dragon. The Olson dragon has twenty . . . twenty-eight lives."

Standing next to Justin, little but a mound of hooded sweatshirt piled on his desk, I saw the outline of his hat and headphones. From Marissa's castle on the mountain, a dizzying sprint to the valley. I pulled out his analysis of the role of friends and confidants in the play from under his elbow.

On the top line, his blue thesis: *This book isn't gay.*

June 10

The end approaches. I'm hoping the final exam will bring together the strands of the year. The prompt: *Save a book on its way to the dump by altering its inside. That is, take an unwanted, unloved paperback or hardback and give it new life by transforming it. Glue, paint, cut, and collage to your heart's content. Keep the binding intact. Reconsider the writing you've done this year and include your best work: two whole pieces of writing, multiple significant excerpts, and as many outstanding sentences as you can reasonably (or unreasonably!) squeeze in the book. Make your presentation visually captivating and mechanically perfect. Make it something you will treasure forever.*

In a flurry of paper, I returned assignments I had stored in a cabinet throughout the year. I passed around manila envelopes with metal clasps to keep everything organized. Only Megan protested. "We're going to write . . . in a book?"

"The janitors are tossing whole stacks of world history textbooks. This is your chance to save one."

"By writing in it?"

"Yes!"

Mason left his envelope on the floor. After what I've done for him—conferencing one-on-one, rummaging through his backpack, stapling his assignments to the wall—I feel invested in the few pages of writing he produced for me. After the bell, I walked out of class, hopped down the patio steps, cut through the tennis courts, and walked past the choir room. Envelope in hand, I skirted the crowd by the main entrance and exited the side doors.

I stood in the bus turnaround holding the envelope and looking at the long line of buses in front of me.

I got on the first bus. "Is Mason Jones here?" I asked.

No response.

I got on buses 13, 19, and 42. "Is Mason Jones here?" Nothing. "Who are you?" one driver asked. Another driver wished me luck.

Passengers on bus 56 must have seen me coming because I heard whooping and hollering as I walked up the steps. I turned my head to the side, scouring the brown seats, stepping over duffel bags and band instruments as I walked to the back. Just past the emergency exit door, I found Mason cowering on the floor next to a wheel bump, with chopsticks in his mouth.

"Here's your work," I said.

"Shhhhhhit," he said through the chopsticks.

"It's not shit," I said, holding out the envelope. "That's why I'm giving it to you. We worked hard to produce these drafts, and we're not going back. Hold on to this envelope, take it home, and don't lose it."

I turned to the students kneeling and standing on their seats around me. "Do not let Mason leave the bus without this envelope," I said.

I gave him the envelope and made my way to the front. "Some days . . ." the bus driver said.

"Some days . . ." I echoed.

June 16

I cannot take any more end-of-the-year pleas for extra credit.

Enough.

You, student, are not here for a gold star or a marble in a jar.

You are not here for bonus bucks, bumper stickers, trophies, certificates, or plaques. You are not here for a piece of candy or the "Good job" your teacher will give you when you jump high enough to get it.

Do not believe in red licorice. The more I reward you, the more you convince yourself you're working for a prize.

Do not accept Tootsie Rolls for being an independent thinker because then you no longer are.

Do not accumulate credentials for the sole purpose of eventually monopolizing success.

School should be more than collecting marks and earning checks.

I know you worked hard to be Student of the Month, and that

you've done a lot as the president of your after-school club. But I'm sorry, I don't think your work should be connected to your parents' love.

I can say that because maybe I know how it feels.

I know, I know. College admissions boards can't see how much you've grown inside without looking at your grades. The gatekeepers count on the systems we have. They makes notes about who came in first and who finished last.

But I'm rooting for everyone in the system who sees beyond the system and pushes past.

So tell me, are you here to be responsible and reflective? To be a member of our community? To be a citizen in a democracy? To think about the world? To think about yourself? To interact with new kinds of people?

You decide.

If you're here for something quantitative or tangible I can provide, like multiple-choice tests to take or lists to memorize, I can't give you anything.

Except maybe if you put a smile on your face and get in line with the other students waiting patiently. Here's how it works. I give them candy bars. They give me their minds.

Look at me, so confident.

"You're weird," I said to first period. They laughed. "No really, you're weird. Do you listen to yourselves? 'Is there a rubric? Is this worth points? When are you going to be entering this assignment in the gradebook?' It's not like I don't understand how you're feeling. I do. I'm the one who rented rock climbing equipment in eleventh grade and scaled the sides of my high school and broke in. I knew Mr. Craftwell had the answers to his final exam hidden somewhere in his desk drawer."

"You did not," Evan said.

"I was looking for the magic formula for acing precalculus," I said. "I knew Mr. Craftwell had it in there . . . but enough about me.

Friday will be the last day to discuss or ask questions about specific assignments."

"Friday's the last day we can ask about grades?" Jacob asked.

"Yes."

"And after that we can't ask?"

"Correct," I said. Sue arched her back. "Most of you work hard," I added. "Keep working hard, and you don't need to worry."

We took a break. Students walked around and pawed the ground with their shoes as if I had buried beneath them something important.

I was a different teacher in fourth and fifth periods. "Half of you are failing," I said to my on-level classes, passing out copies of itemized progress reports. "I like you, but you're failing. And I want you to pass this class." I distributed markers and asked students to underline missing assignments. I asked them to list the assignments in their planners. "We have one more big project between now and the end of the year," I said, "and it's going to be worth a lot of points. I want you to talk with me between now and Friday about your grade, so we can make sure you'll pass."

So. The Points Factory is closed in first and second periods but open and ready for business in the afternoons. Perhaps my philosophy on grades should be consistent. Perhaps the odd hours of the Point Factory says something about my underlying convictions. As much as Paton is a chameleon—keeping the aisles clear during class and humping the soda machine after school—I'm a chameleon.

June 17

The clouds gathered around the mountain like tourists around great art. The rest of the sky was clear and blue. I hauled my kayak down to the water and paddled farther than I'd ever been. Mount Rainier looked stately in the distance. Hundreds of sand dollars formed a craggy, purple carpet of five-petal discs below me. Every ripple from my paddle made the cilia on the sand dollars sway. I looked to the west, balanced my paddle on the cockpit, and reclined in the plastic seat.

I should be as vibrant as the sun, I thought.

I want my students to be alive and growing. I want them to think through ideas with precision. Are they doing that? *Have* they done it? I'm finally ready to ask myself the question Principal Pike asked me, in so many words, before I was ready to hear it: you work hard, but are your students getting what they need?

Our whole-group conversations have gotten better. "To add on to what Cameron said . . .," Jenna says. Or, "I see it differently than Jessy sees it. I'm probably 70/30 in favor of . . .," Pam qualifies. Students say thank you when I distribute papers. David brought me a cell phone that doesn't work anymore because he dropped it in a toilet. He said he wanted me to add the parts to my wind chime of broken cells.

I wake up every morning and put on my teacher clothes. I act like a teacher. I mostly feel like a teacher.

I sat upright in my kayak and looked out at the sky reflected across the water. I angled my face toward the eye of the sun. Veteran teachers say, "Don't worry, just give yourself the year," as if I could for one second believe my students were nothing more than subjects in a beginning teacher's yearlong trial run. If I'm going to forgive myself for the mistakes I've made this year, I need to be clear about the ethics of the research. The control group and the experimental group have been one and the same.

Gripping my paddle and reaffirming my belief in functional grace, I pushed toward a place on shore where driftwood gathered around a madrona tree like chairs around a pulpit at a start-up church. When the bottom of the kayak scraped the beach, I stepped out and dragged it on shore, wedging it between two boulders.

Heading to my left, I found a trail overgrown with ferns and blackberries. After twenty or thirty steps across an embankment, the trail flattened and merged with another path. The widened path became an open, logged corridor where telephone poles repeated and yellow flowers bloomed. I thought about the trucks that must have rattled along this path to clear out the trees and the workers who erected the poles. This is how my laptop charges at home while I'm kayaking Puget Sound and walking trails outside.

How much can I take in? Or give?

How sensitive can I be to the light?

I stood on the trail asking myself these questions for twenty or thirty minutes. The answers, I think, have as much to do with the battery in my laptop as with the projector bulb in my classroom. Typing sentences about my life on my computer is important to my teaching life because I'm figuring out how to say, in so many words, this is how I'm learning to get out of the way.

Grass Stays a Healthy Green

Department meeting in Elaina's room. We arranged seven desks in a circle and shared our summer plans. Janet said she's applying for a job at the district where she will hopefully work with other teachers to build, or maybe buy from a company, an articulated, guaranteed Language Arts curriculum.

"Guaranteed?" I asked.

"Teacher-proof," Alice said. "Like a workbook."

"All track team members to the front of the school," the track coach interrupted on the school's intercom. "All track team members to the front of the school."

"Everyone in the same grade will do the same thing?" I asked.

"Teacher-proof is like idiot-proof," Alice said.

"Bellevue has had great success with the program we're thinking about adopting," Elaina said. "There's power to be found in horizontal and vertical alignment . . . but let's keep going. What are you doing this summer, Derek?"

"Attending a journalism conference," I said, "and I might stay with my parents for a while and work on a farm."

"You'll love being outside," Elaina said. "I'm going to read murder myst—"

"Make sure you create a final exam," Principal Pike interrupted, standing in the doorway. "I'm stopping by to make sure you all give a final exam. Last year we had teachers—"

"Also, Hawk Hoops will begin at 2:30. Again, Hawk Hoops begins at 2:30."

"—and I thought I'd give a reminder."

We ordered supplies. Elaina, Janet, and I asked for 0.2 mm pens for grading. Everyone requested new Swingline staplers, dry erase markers, and rolls of butcher paper. Elaina asked us to write down our dream schedules for next year. I requested ninth-grade English.

June 19

After students spent a week working on their altered books and I received several reports of projects taking over bedroom floors and kitchen tables, students handed in their final exams. I collected four boxes of books, about a hundred and fifteen projects in all. So far, I've graded seventeen. I said I'd give each book ten minutes, but the reality so far is more like twenty. In presenting their best writing, students used charcoal, pastel, watercolor, acrylic, coffee grounds, and grass. Darrell sewed a handwritten reader's contract into the binding of his book. Pippa included a poem and a pair of earrings in an afterword called "Jewelry & Accessories."

The first page of Mason's book is black Sharpie on white paper: *Due to my lack of creativity the following will be an ebony and ivory gallery.*

For those of you who don't know me, his second page starts, *and those of you who don't wanna know me (shame on you, I'm a very loveable and respectable human being), I have conducted a survey on myself.*

Age: 16 going on 9.

Occupation: student, ex-convict.

Favorite food: Mr. Smith Soup, Silence of the Lambs-style.

Hobbies: women, books, eating, pretending my life has meaning, and pillows yaaaaaaa!

Would like to visit: white sand beach with mirror-like purple ocean settling below the gaze of three gibbous moons.

Page three: *The following bit of writing will be done by hand. I am doing this book and doing it very quickly because I have a very low attention span. After a bit of thinking I've come to a conclusion. I'm going to rewrite it all. That's right, you heard me. Everything has got to go.*

He included nothing from the manila envelope.

I like "My Law is Absolute Mortal Law," a list of rules he wants plants, animals, and people to follow on his imaginary planet. *Every tree will grow a different type of fruit and/or flower*, he writes. *Every day you will have a new name of your choosing (you can borrow someone else's name but there will be a name transaction fee). Snakes kiss instead of bite. Cheese never spoils. Hamburgers will no longer be called hamburgers but burgers. Grass stays a healthy green no matter the circumstance. All words I make up are real words.*

My favorite page contains an allegory about climbing a mountain: *The Wanderer looked at The Mountain and at the vein-violet squall on the horizon. Clouds hovered over him like giant praying mantises. It was his destination, his only destination. Flexing his limbs and adjusting his rucksack, he ventured up the winding path.*

This is how the book ends: *As I awoke from my dream, I cursed the creak in my spring mattress and rose to an upright position. I placed my sweaty feet in the only clean spot on the ground. Apes beat drums between my ears like red-hot lances on the soft part of my brain. Light broke through the curtains like a barrage of javelins from the sky.*

Onto Celina's book. A note tucked in the front reads, *I know you said this was due whether we were here today or not, so I brought it by on my way to visit my mom in the hospital.*

The beginning: *One dark day when I was sad, it started to rain rubies. I got up to get a key to go to the bathroom, and the key was connected to a bundle of plastic roses. When I opened the bathroom door, a red carpet led me to an ocean.*

The middle includes a story with blacked out names and pronouns. Opposite the story, a blurry family photo. *This is a picture of me and my mother*, the caption reads. *As you can see, it is out of focus. This is how our relationship is.*

She ends with her eulogy. *Celina was always thinking, even when it was unnecessary. It took her longer than necessary to answer simple yes and no questions.*

June 20

The altered book grading marathon continues.

What I like so far, Megan writes, *is rebelling against my head*. That's after some thoughts on the *unending process of testing* and a plea for her generation to live in the moment. *We do not need tomorrow's plans to make us happy*, she writes. *We have been conditioned from birth to live with the incentive of the excitement of the future. I catch myself saying, "I'm in a good mood because this weekend will be fun." I think we need to realize life is beautiful even in the midst of our so-called "boredom."*

Like Mason, she produced new material:
I wonder what it's like to
be the prettiest word in the
English language
whatever that may be
with a fan club somewhere;
a group of high school kids sitting at a lunch table
when someone brings up the question:
"Hey guys, what's your favorite word?"
and everyone thinks awhile
and someone says the name of the prettiest word
and everyone agrees
and is quiet.

She included six copies of a mix CD in a side pocket with directions that say, *Take one. Write me a letter and tell me what you think.* She also says she would like to meet all the people who appear in her dreams, even pirates, because where pirates live, anything is possible. No scissors were used in the making of her book because the project made her feel more torn than cut.

Farah wrote, *There came a day when I couldn't take it anymore. My father hit me with a broom handle while his girlfriend held me down. I always believed my dad was going to stand by me and even now I don't know why he chose his girlfriend over his daughter. Before she came into our lives my father was a role model. We worked on our bikes together. We went shopping and camping together. I was his girl. I never dreamed one day I'd call the cops on him. I didn't want him to leave. But now I have an emotional shield, and it helps me from being weak.*

The first page of David's book is a headshot of David wearing a polo shirt. He stares into the camera, unsmiling. His right hand scratches the top of his head, like he's figuring something out. His hair fans out over his ears.

Printed above the picture: *I did this for me.*

Below the picture: *And nobody else.*

The rest of the page is empty.

On the second page he included part of a book report he never turned in and a story about discussing religion with drunk people at a party in which the narrator realizes the people at the party probably don't understand the complexity of his ideas. The rest of the book is the rest of the book, unaltered.

One philosophy of grading is that failing grades should be reserved for students who complete assignments but fall substantially below the standard. David didn't even complete the assignment. He never tried.

David is like teachers who guarantee themselves feelings of success by saying they'll teach students who want to learn. If students don't want to learn, these teachers say, well then, they can't be taught. These teachers never try to teach unmotivated students, so they never technically fail.

June 21

It's 4:45 p.m. The vents in my classroom have stopped pumping air. I'm staring in disbelief at my computer. Unless I fudge the numbers,

David will get a C– in my class. His revenge on all of us will be a passing grade.

I've considered lowering the grade to a D or an F. After all, I've been changing grades on progress reports all year long. If a student who turns in assignments and has been showing effort falls in the range of 60 to 63 percent, I generally bump up the grade to 64 percent, a D. That's what I've been allowing, a percent or two, maybe three.

For me, the gradebook is a backup, a check for what I already know about students' knowledge and growth. Despite what teachers say ("Well, if we look here, the gradebook shows . . ."), gradebooks are not objective. Who says a poem is worth ten points or one hundred points? I do. Who decides the point total for each semester? I do. Teachers can grade by averaging test scores, totaling median scores, adding total points, or deleting lowest scores. Every method yields different results. I could have made the altered book project worth half of the total for the entire year (and I suppose I still could), but I didn't (and I won't) because I'm aiming for my students' grades to be as meaningful as possible.

I fish out a popcorn fragment from between the space bar and the alt key.

David should fail the altered book project for having too little writing. He should get a D for the class overall.

I told myself when I started changing grades I would move numbers up but never down.

David gets a Cocky and a Careless.

In other news, Mason has a 38 percent.

Mason, the young man who claims Hermes's sandals are not "aerodynamically correct" and describes sadness as the sound of crayons melting in a dryer, is about to fail. Can I give him credit for starting the Hallway Philosophy Club and for hiding behind my door and doing a popsicle stick puppet show through the little window? "Mr. Smith!" a bow-tied puppet said. "I have a theory about God I want to share!"

In a different time and place, Mason might succeed. But we're in Gig Harbor, Washington, at the start of the new millennium. An A from Peninsula High has to compare to an A from Somewhere Else.

I scan the grades. There's Megan, the bearer of the torch, leading the way out of the cave; David, the sham artist on the path of least resistance; Mason, the self-assigned curricular anarchist; Justin, the academically misplaced wannabe thug; and Farah, the wildflower pushing through a crack in concrete.

Technically, I should have checked in with Justin's special education teacher to see if he had been retested and if his accommodations have changed, but with his number of absences, I can't imagine it would matter.

Megan, David, Mason, Justin, Farah, and 115 more.

In the end, some of them get what's coming to them. Some of them don't.

Megan: A.

David: C−.

Mason: F.

Justin: F.

Farah: C+.

I click on Mason's row. I find the largest missing assignment and change it to an A. Sixty-four percent. Mason will pass with a D.

June 22

"Some of you will leave here remembering the concepts we learned, the ideas we talked about, and the conversations we shared," I said to first period. "Some of you will leave and remember the projects you completed. Some of you will remember one thing: your grade.

"Some of you have As because you played the game," I continued. "Some of you have Cs because you worked hard and brought your best and loved discussing ideas with the group more than you loved meeting deadlines.

"All of you inspired me to be a better teacher. We had our ups and downs, but you were always earnest and honest about your learning."

First period cleaned the room. We took down the Queen Mab renderings from *Romeo and Juliet*, the eulogies from *Fahrenheit 451*, the poems about magazine advertisements, the wall-length Slaughter in the Hall poster and ODY.FM radio station sign. Behind everything was a reading strategies poster spotted with mold.

"Take your work home," I said, "or leave it. Don't touch the mold."

"He's going to hate the eighth graders," Sarah called over the sounds of crinkling paper.

"They're horrible," Katy said.

"Should I get these?" Micaela asked. She stood on a desk by the *To Kill A Mockingbird* cartoons stapled to the ceiling.

We never read *To Kill A Mockingbird*. One more item for the We Never list. We never practiced persuasive writing. We never studied Latin roots. We never took a spelling walk. I never wrote Idaho Girl another letter.

"Leave those," I said.

"What about the countdown to the first day of school?"

"I just put that up!" I said. "We have seventy-nine days to get ready for fall."

A small group huddled around my desk. Jacob, Kevin, and Marc asked if they could haul the filing cabinet to the dumpster since Murray was never able to find the key. When I nodded, they tipped it sideways and watched it fall to the floor. They tried picking it up. When they failed, they sat on it sideways and called out for help. Pam, Katy, Christy, Paton, and Evan asked if they could join the journalism club.

I asked each class where they wanted to take their class picture. First period chose the parking lot. Second period chose the bleachers. Fourth period lined up along the patio railing. Fifth period stood in front of a dumpster with the words *Homework sucks* spray-painted on the side.

I returned their altered books and explained the meaning of the star stickers: green stars were for anecdotes that showed personality, blue stars were for sentence structures that corresponded to the content or message of the writing, red stars indicated inspired arguments, silver stars signaled superb figurative language, and gold stars were there to shine on unexpected moments of magic or mystery.

A few minutes before the bell, I told fifth period they were my "earthquake class."

"You want us to die?" Farah asked.

"Smith wants us to die," Grant said.

"If we had an earthquake, and I had to be at school for an indefinite amount of time with a group of students, I'd choose you," I said.

"You say that to all your classes," Marissa said.

"Second period is his lockdown class," Josh added.

"Third period is his flood class," Derrell added.

"I didn't say that," I said.

RIIILNNNNNNGGGGGG.

Students jumped out of their seats. I stood by the door and gave them high fives as they streamed off the patio. Some students yelled, "Paper fight!" A student from another class balanced a recycling bin on his head as he ran past the tennis courts. "What's going on?" I asked.

"Paper fight," Grant said. "Can I have the recycling?"

I shut the door and followed the mob past the tennis courts, down the stairs, past the gym and Principal Pike's office, and into the cafeteria where I stood by the à la carte and watched folders, planners, protractors, pencil pouches, and spiral notebooks fly through the air and land on a tile floor that, back in September, had sparkled like a lake. Dividers, flashcards, and loose paper. An altered book, a mouse pad, a pair of gym shorts. A boy executed a showy snowboarding move on a three-ring binder while mugging for his friends' phones.

The scene was not unlike the punk rock, antiauthoritarian music videos I had, on several occasions, feared my fifth period would turn into. I hoped no one overturned tables.

Murray and three other custodians leaned against pop machines with black garbage bags in their hands. I leaned over to Alice. "Does this happen every year?" I asked.

"Every year," she said. "Tradition."

I wished Alice a good summer and walked to my room. Outside my door I found a book wrapped in brown butcher paper with a note on the front.

I want to know your favorite parts. But don't think you have to write back or anything—you can just tell me next year. I love that every book Charlie reads becomes his favorite, just like me. Thanks for everything!
—M

I unwrapped the book and found more writing around the edges of the butcher paper: *I wish my eyes and hands could be more connected . . . COMPASSION . . . I wish that when someone cries in front of other people, instead of everyone becoming awkward, everyone would start crying too. For the same reason or for reasons of their own.*

I went inside and closed the door.

I drew the blinds over the pink rhododendrons.

Light breaks through the curtains like a barrage of javelins from the sky.

Knockknockknock.

I was on the floor.

Knockknockknock.

Wiping tears from my eyes, I got up. Adam and Grant stood there with three or four stacks of sticky notes.

"We found them in our backpacks and thought you might like them," Grant said. There was a small stick person drawn on top of one of the stacks of sticky notes.

"We stole them a long time ago," Adam said.

"We almost threw them away in the paper fight," Grant added. "Adam drew the stick figures."

"Do you want them back?" Adam asked, holding out the stacks for me.

I took the top stack and flipped through the pages. The stick figure brought his arms over his head and his legs apart, doing jumping jacks. The stack ended on a high note, with the man suspended in mid-air, feet off the ground.

By the time I looked up, Adam was teasing Grant about something, pointing at his light-up shoes.

"I need them for running through your girlfriend's mind," Grant replied. "It's dark in there."

"Thanks, guys," I said. "I'm glad you brought these to me. Don't steal from your teachers next year."

They smiled and ran across the patio, returning to the cafeteria paper fight.

I hauled the copies of *Romeo and Juliet* to the bookroom, tucking Claire and Leo into their tomb.

I set my out-of-office auto-reply: *Derek Smith is outside learning something new. He will return to the office in late August.*

I leaned back in my desk chair, considering the grand task my colleagues and I had accomplished this year, spending so much time sequestered in our classrooms, and now, suddenly, free.

I can breathe, I thought. *I can clean the coffee pot with a wadded-up paper towel and hold the pot to the light to check the cleanliness.*

Gazing out the window and across the tennis courts and football field, I lifted the lid on the diorama of the school I had created in my mind's eye over the course of the year.

In one corner of the diorama, in a room with a desk and three beds, the school nurse stacked ice packs on a shelf.

In another corner, in the kitchen, the head cook hung aluminum pots on a wall.

Another room over, the school psychiatrist pushed documents through a paper shredder.

Elsewhere, a PE teacher tied a knot in the top of a mesh bag of soccer balls, a history teacher stumbled toward a dumpster with a stack of trifold poster boards, and a track coach added a hurdle to a row of hurdles under the bleachers.

Three students in football jerseys leaned on the bumpers of their cars, hands tucked into their belts like cowboys.

A world history teacher in N-3 pulled paper Chinese dragons off the wall. A math teacher in N-5 pushed a Pythagorean doghouse into an already full cupboard. An English teacher in N-7 inched his keyboard closer to his chest.

This is how I tell the story of my time.

The teacher looked at the projector in the front of the room.

Each day, I stand by a projector, lesson plan in hand.

He looked at the desks stacked off to the side.

When I step away from the projector, I step toward my students.

The carpet was strewn with staples. A metal spiral by the trash can looked like a worm on a sidewalk. The teacher looked at his empty room. It was time for him to save his work, swing his bag over his shoulder, and put his hands on the light switches one last time.

June 24

I read through the course evaluations.

What did you learn? What did you like?

I learned that even things that seem lame can be fun if you're bold enough to try.

How to write sentences.

I like that I feel like a better person because of your class.

I could tell that you wanted to be here every day and wanted to teach. Keep that attitude in the future.

Everyone gets involved, most of the time by free will.

Our class is weird, and by "weird" I mean "unorthodox." We string chains of sticky notes from the ceiling. We write papers. And then we abandon them until several months later. One time we took over the class. Mr. Smith says he "only pretends to teach English," which is only partly true. We learn English, and we also learn life lessons.

You act like a teacher but don't talk like one, if that makes sense.

You were always here and always dressed up. The only time I didn't see you dressed up was when you were in Target!

I think you will be a very good teacher. You caught the people that cheated most of the time.

What would you change?

Not enough fun or movies.

Probably have us work in small groups like two people at most because bigger groups are sloppy.

I think you were aware of what was going on, but in my opinion I think you could be more strict.

You probably know this is coming, but you're a first-year teacher. You shouldn't be so strict. Make your kids say, "Mr. Smith is cool."

I think you should have done the spelling walk, and you should do the talking in third-person point of view lesson too.

Participation points riiiggggghhht?

The best thing you can do is keep changing the tone, pitch, and volume of your voice. When you teach, you fling your arms, open your eyes, stutter, and stammer over your words in excitement to convey a point.

What advice would you give to a student next year?

Whenever you get a writing assignment, write and write and write. Write a lot, even if it doesn't seem like there is anything more to write.

His gray eyes will get into your soul, and you will be trapped in a barren wasteland of perpetual winter.

Mr. Smith can seem scary, but when you get further into the school year, he's actually pretty cool if you do your assignments and don't throw markers out the window.

Mr. Smith will probably get in your head a lot because he sure did get in mine, but if you finish your work strong then in the end he does his cheer and he screams, which is a relief after he gets on your case. This class is chilled, hard, fun, and time consuming. Just add your own spice and everything will go fine, and oh, Mr. Smith loves yogurt-covered pretzels and yogurt-covered almonds mixed in a bag, so if you manage to get on his bad side, just toss him a bag of that mix, and you'll be in the clear. One time Mr. Smith was mad at me, and I gave him a bag of that mix, and he told me, "How can I hate you now?!" Ahhhhhhhhhh yup! To be honest I was really trying to be a nice guy and give him a treat with no intentions on raising the good bar with him, just because I knew his love for little snacks. Well that's my final thoughts so good luck.

Fifteen Years Later

I sit crisscross-applesauce on the brown carpet of my apartment floor, typing these sentences as I recall my teaching career. Fifteen years isn't long by some standards, but I've got piles of ephemerae around me testifying to the time I've spent working with young people so far: stacks of assignments students left behind or didn't want, notes I scrawled on the backs of surplus handouts during the school day, old meeting agendas. I started working on this book in October, going through journal entries from my first year of teaching and recalling that first eclectic cohort. In the process, I've been going through everything I've kept ever since.

My former department chair used to say teachers need summertime to give themselves Fs like friends, family, fitness, and foolishness. Summer, she said, is when teachers go wild, or at least let loose. Summer is when we nurture the fundamental parts of our lives we may have neglected during the school year. For me, that means writing more. And I have been. I've been writing for pleasure on topics like faith, Olympic figure skating, the Fibonacci sequence, the fulcrum between geography and gender, and my father.

And, of course, school.

....

"As a rule, people don't celebrate the middle of things," *Esquire* fashion director Nick Sullivan wrote in an article about finding good men's clothes in Kansas in 2015. "They celebrate the edges, the beginnings and the ends: births, christenings, marriages, graduations. Even death carries with it a stronger sense of occasion than any bit in the middle."[8] Psychological research supports Sullivan's notion. People remember the first and last items in a series more than anything in between. Plot graphs in literature courses reinforce it: people want rising and falling action, exposition and denouement.

That said, the frame of primacy and recency is little without something inside it. The illuminated menu at Subway highlights what goes between slices of bread. We live for the twenty minutes at the holiday party when everybody has arrived but no one is feeling the urge to leave. Great things happen in the middle.

Maybe I'm looking for reasons to be okay with my decision to accept a job at a middle school rather than sitting with the sadness I felt about the dreams that never materialized when I left Renton High three years ago. I applied for communications and PR jobs almost every day. I interviewed for a position editing product descriptions on a baby clothing website. I hoofed through community college hallways and introduced myself to faculty.

I didn't know what my next step would be. I had given up my job teaching high school because I felt compelled to move on. Part of me imagined I would climb the ranks of academia and advance to teaching college classes, starting with bread-and-butter courses like English 101 and English 102 for a few years. Once I got my feet under me, I would settle into upper-level seminars. My typical lesson would involve introducing competing philosophical frames on a whiteboard and then opening the floor for discussion.

But no.

---

[8] Nick Sullivan, "I Was Dropped in the Middle of Kansas in Nothing But My Underwear," *Esquire*, August 2015.

I now teach middle school. I spend my days in what some educators refer to as the armpit of education. There aren't too many kickoffs or opening numbers, perfect dismounts or encores. In middle school, we focus on the "art of paragraphing" with excruciating exactitude. Given that this last school year was my third year of teaching sixth grade—fifteen years after those first reality checks and bursts of adrenaline with my freshmen at Peninsula High—maybe I shouldn't have been so quick to call the concluding paragraph in the final essay I graded at Renton High the Last Paragraph.

I don't know what life has in store. Contemplating the possibility that I might teach until I retire, I realize I have a few years before I reach the halfway point of my career. I've learned so much already. What will I learn as I make my way through the middle myself? If I'm going to keep teaching, I want the intermediate junctures along the continuum, the imminent U-turns and detours and loopty loops, to be as important as the beginning and ending points, maybe even more important if they involve my favorite middletons, eleven- and twelve-year-olds.

I'm thinking back to the first day of school last September. Groups of sixth-grade students entered through the clocktower doors. When they got to the main hall, they ran back and forth to show each other their lockers. They double-checked their schedules. Teachers milled about and reminded students to use their "walking feet." We offered greetings like "We've been waiting for you."

As a get-to-know-you activity, I asked my homeroom students, "What's the strangest talent you have?" When I turned around and faced the class after writing the question on the whiteboard, I saw a veritable vaudeville: six or seven disjointed thumbs, a boy with his legs tucked behind his head, a girl doing a pirouette, three pairs of crossed eyes, and something called "the vibrating pupils trick."

"Wow, look at you," I said, taking it all in. "Here's the second question. What are three things you're grateful for?"

"To be going to McKnight," the boy with vibrating pupils said, "and that my soul is inside my body, and that my feet have the pleasure of walking the earth."

The girl who had pirouetted but had since landed in a position with her arms cradled and heels touching, shouted, "I got to read a funny book this morning, and this afternoon we're going to a pep assembly. Today is the best day!"

Later during the period, while students planned their walking routes for the day on photocopied school maps, John walked up to me and pointed to a red circle on his face. "I had to vacuum the house," he explained, "because I got in trouble for asking Alexa to order our grandma an Alexa. And then I got in trouble for sticking the vacuum hose on my chin."

"A dependence on technology can isolate you from your inner self," Cynthia warned him from across the room.

As a group and by themselves, middle school students are a medley of maturity. I confiscate cell phones. I confiscate flour-filled balloons and containers of slime. One morning last fall, an administrator emailed me to say she suspended a boy for selling vape pens on campus. I knew him as the boy who sang "Pancake Robot" and "There's a Cat Licking Your Birthday Cake" during clean-up time at the end of the day. Shaina came out as transgender in mid-November, saying he preferred male pronouns but would need a few months to decide on a name. I later caught him trying to levitate a pencil that had rolled off his desk. After a minute of holding his hands out like claws, he rolled his eyes and bent down to retrieve the pencil, clearly disappointed. Two books were on his desk: an animal fantasy in which cats talk to each other and a book about domestic violence. Shaina's writing vacillates as much from fanciful to forthright as his reading, and my students' writing as a whole is as assorted as Shaina's: ready and reluctant, simple and sophisticated.

Manny, for example, began his persuasive essay on a social issue with this claim: *If you skip breakfast, you will not go to college.*

Have you ever wanted to stay on something really bad, like a toy horse? Laurel wrote at the start of her argument about the Dakota Access Pipeline. *Well, the Native Americans want to stay on their land.*

Cynthia wrote about immigration reform. *If asylum seekers flowing from the Arab world could be allowed to enter other Middle Eastern nations, child refugees would not have to learn a new language and could continue growing up in a Muslim-majority country*, she wrote. *The US may not be the best option.*

I remove a binder clip from a stack of personal narratives and look through the papers. I recall the assignment and how students embraced the request to write honestly about their lives.

Zitlaly wrote about a family emergency. *We got to the hospital around three o'clock*, she wrote. *We looked like we were going camping because we had so many backpacks and blankets for my dad and mom.*

You could say I was bouncing off the walls, Ivette wrote, *but I was actually bouncing between my bed and my sister's bed continuously.*

Meanwhile, Paisley wrote, *All I remember was jumping into my great idea and landing with a splash.*

Lennon described an emotional release, admitting that, *Beating up a soap dispenser is really satisfying actually.*

Judge me how you want for playing a videogame from 2010, Stephen started, *but that's where my story begins.*

One day a kid was walking out of school while he was being bullied, Bradley wrote. *Now it's summer vacation.*

I called Bradley and Reese over to my desk. "Bradley, I love how you've laid out the beginning and end of your story," I said. "This means you're ready for the next step: developing the middle."

"Reese," I continued, "will you tell Bradley what you told me before class? About the middle part of your book?"

"I'm at the best-worst part," Reese said, "and I really want to find out what happens next, but I don't. I think the author is hiding some of what he knows."

Students endured round after round of revision where they re-considered a moment from their lives through the lenses of beginning, middle, and end. When all was said and done, we pushed our desks into a circle and shared our strongest excerpts. "It was cold enough to see my own breath," Ren recalled, describing a visit with his bio-logical dad, "but I knew the fog would evaporate the way people do."

When everyone was done sharing, students held their pouches of Capri Sun in the air and gave a toast to the work they had done and the courage they had summoned to read aloud even when it was scary. We called it a Toast to Bravery. I couldn't call it a Toast to Change, after all—since that idea comes from *Freedom Writers*, a movie I once dismissed as lofty and corny.

I switch how my legs are crossed on the living room carpet, lean forward, and pick up Maxine Greene's *The Dialectic of Freedom* from my bookshelf. I turn to a dog-eared page: "An education for free-dom must move beyond function, beyond the subordination of per-sons to external ends."[9] I pick up Paulo Freire's *Pedagogy of the Op-pressed* and flip through it. "Any situation in which some men pre-vent others from engaging in the process of inquiry," he writes, "is one of violence."[10]

I shut my eyes. I imagine, for a moment, I'm back in N-7 at Pen-insula High. I'm back in my fifth-period freshman English class, my earthquake class. Students rock back and forth in their chairs. Grant and Adam talk about daily double math. When they tire of rocking, they work together side by side, like two parts of a compound word. I imagine myself walking to the faculty lunchroom after school, where

---

[9] Maxine Greene, *The Dialectic of Freedom* (New York: Teachers College Press, 2018), 132-133.

[10] Paulo Freire, *Pedagogy of the Oppressed* (New York: The Continuum Interna-tional Publishing Group, Inc., 2005), 85.

I open the freezer and pull out a half-eaten sheet cake leftover from a recognition banquet. I dig around in the back. The pile of Otter Pops is still there.

I imagine I'm back at Renton High. My second-period juniors are discussing metaphors for the Internet. Alison says surfing the web is like riding a jet ski because we speed along the surface of topics we should know more about, like Darfur. Jamil says the perimeter of our knowledge is ever increasing but the inside is vaporous. At some point everything is going to pop. Kenneth says our conversation depresses him. Human beings are pancake people, and that's that.

I imagine McKnight Middle, and I think about Mateo, one of last year's smallest sixth-grade students. With the school counselor's help, he called an after-school meeting with his teachers because he wanted us to know he sometimes gets hit with a ruler "all over" but that "it's not abuse because it doesn't leave a mark." A few of us who had called home earlier in the year about Mateo's missing work looked across the table at each other with pained expressions, fearing what we had done.

When I think about how much Mateo would love Mason's Hallway Philosophy Club, I start to wonder what Mason is up to these days. I wonder if he still takes up the cause of subverting institutions. I wonder what rules he has about teachers joining his club, and if there might be a branch or sect for educators working within the grids he circumvented with such delight.

I imagine the future of magical teaching belongs in part to people like Mason. He considered but wasn't controlled by what he learned from books, television shows, and films. He relished the act of imagining.

I look through the course evaluations my sixth graders completed on the last day of class. In the space on the back, I asked students to draw a picture of their summer plans. Cassidy drew a picture of herself clearing plates at her family's restaurant. Wes drew a picture of himself dyeing his hair alongside the entirety of the swimming team. Luciana drew a portrait of her family in a brick courtyard in Guadalajara. Three family members hold musical instruments: a trombone, a trumpet, and a guitar.

I encouraged students without summer plans to draw x-rays of their backpacks. Gabriel's backpack held Nike Mercurial Vapor soccer cleats. Phoenix's backpack contained a Yu-Gi-Oh! deck, an iPhone XS Max, and Benjamin Alire Sáenz's *Aristotle and Dante Discover the Secrets of the Universe*. Kaci's backpack contained a Sakura-Con key chain, a small glass cylinder filled with her mother's ashes, and eye paint leftover from a pep assembly.

As I look through their backpack sketches, I recall my students flinging their candy-stripe suitcases every which way on that imaginary grassy knoll on the mountain, *Sound of Music*-style. To this day, I strive for that kind of warmth and whimsy in my classroom. When I don't achieve it, I settle for the slog, the scene in which my students line up on the snowy mountain ridge with their backpacks.

Caves dot the mountainside. I've got two students with me, Wes and Kaci. It's a few years in the future. Wes says he's sad because he's been locked out of the doc his friends use for group chatting. Kaci says she's been reading an autobiography by one of her favorite lesbian videographers as an antidote to PE.

We've been making our way across this mountain for the better part of the year, checking out different caves as we go. We try not to look too much at the castle on the peak.

We pass the detention cave, where we overhear a student say he cusses in front of Mrs. Pagotto because he likes to watch her reach up and touch her neck in shock. "Can you imagine Mrs. Pagotto in an active killer response drill?" he asks his friend one desk over. "Defending our class with her little bottle of hand sanitizer?"

"I'm tired of this mountain," Wes says. "Where should we go next?"

"Let's go there," Kaci says, pointing to another mountain.

"You don't want to go there?" I ask, pointing to the castle on the mountain we've been ascending. "The clouds are finally rolling away."

"No, I want to go there," she says, pointing across the valley. In the distance, a massif pokes the sky. Clouds gather around the tallest mountain like spheres around a perfect pyramid.

"It's going to be harder than walking laps around the gym," Wes says. "We could stay here and rest."

"I know," Kaci says. "But you asked, 'Where else?' and I'm telling you."

Fearing the sepia tones of summer might be melting my brain into nostalgia-infused sludge, I remind myself of what the day-to-day is like with regular students. I remember what one of my students told me last year, that some days in school are like "campsite rocks that are too small to sit on but too big to move." I remind myself that in a few weeks I'll leave behind the pleasures that exist in the liminal space between "last year" and "next year."

Next year, I'm guessing, will be somewhat like last year. I'll spend more time than necessary adding conscious hip-hop to my after-school playlist. The subset of students who stay after the bell will ask about my car, and one student will want to know if the wheels are dipped. I'll lose binder clips. Twice during the year I'll step into the hallway and tell my colleagues I'm all caught up. Those will be the only two times I'll be all caught up. I'll survive administrivia from district mucky mucks. I'll show my students the different ways I've been collecting ideas for the lessons we do in class because if I want them to be able to make sense of the world by finding meaning in the flashing lights and noise, I need to show them it's possible.

I'll refrain from looking at my students like they are the embodied grassroots solution to human extinction. I'll insist that we can all be part of the answer. I'll try to imagine being a young person at a time when school officials advise against going door-to-door for the cookie dough fundraiser because the neighborhood is too scary but provide every student with a computer that can access vast swaths of the world's information. I'll try to remember the difference between accommodating students' changing cognitive profiles by letting them work on computers and contributing to the changes myself by letting them work on computers too long. I'll miss the old dance about whether to give James a pencil as my colleagues debate whether kids need pencils at all.

When the holidays come around, I'll send my family members a link to a shopping cart stocked with industrial-strength hole-punchers and fine-point grading pens.

Surely, at some point the ain't-it-awful teacher down the hall will sigh during lunch and break out what Esmé Raji Codell calls The List: "'counselor, mother, friend . . .' on and on."[11] Recounting her work-related duties, she'll lay on her bed of nails like a chaise lounge. "I am a counselor, a secretary, an entertainer, a guide, a confidante, a hallway monitor, and a babysitter," she'll say, "an English teacher but also a teacher of consumer awareness, drug and alcohol prevention, conflict mediation, keyboarding, Internet safety, and social-emotional learning; an arbiter of morality, a harbinger of hope, an apostle of realism, and a mandated reporter; a lice inspector, a censor of T-shirts, and an evangelist of deodorant."

I'll stay late when I have to, and I'll try not to fall from my perch on the filing cabinet while stapling student work to the walls.

Students will typecast teachers because that's partially what students do—go from class to class and hang out for a while with the renegade art teacher in Converse, the *Simpsons*-loving history teacher with

---

[11] Esmé Raji Codell, *Educating Esmé: Diary of a Teacher's First Year* (Chapel Hill: Algonquin Books of Chapel Hill, 2009), 161.

a knack for trivia, the band director who overestimates his power, the coach who covers the walls of his classroom with vintage basketball jerseys, and the English teacher who collects rubber stamps and uses a stuffed animal for a bathroom pass. In return, my colleagues will occasionally let loose in the teacher's lounge and call kids squeaky wheels, fence sitters, and point junkies. I'll groan about my stage four Cling-On, a budding science-fiction writer who updates me every morning on the plot of the book he has yet to start writing.

This harmless boilerplate and low-level gossip won't mean my colleagues' hearts are in the wrong place or that our students are headed in the wrong direction. It will mean that people in my building like to laugh and that there are a lot of people in my building, most of whom don't have much time.

When we have a minute, though, someone will tell a story, and the story will remind us that in environments where uniform ways of looking at people are profoundly engrained, we must look and listen for distinguishing details. Teachers must be among the first to see with precision because we're in charge. We model how to see and interact with people around us in nuanced ways even when our students see us as simply as geeks who lean on windowsills and eat streusel while marking papers. Who knows what kidult, what adultescent, what member of the Remix Generation or Generation Rx or iGen or Generation Wii, might walk into our classrooms with possibilities in mind and questions to scrawl on the walls of our caves?

In many ways, next year won't be like last year. Every year, every student, is original. Last year a boy who had accused me of ruining his five-year streak of writing for his English teachers on the topic of sharks appeared in my classroom doorway. He said he had left his backpack in another room and wanted to know if I had "the universal key."

"You have no idea," I said, looking up from my streusel, "how much I want to say yes."

I stretch out my legs on the living room carpet and pick up my coffee. Here's to my students working hard most of the time, especially given the number of interruptions, the late arrivals and early dismissals for field trips and wrestling matches, orthodontist's and doctor's appointments, speech and SPED screenings.

Here's to finding an old-fashioned doughnut flattened inside a napkin in the supplies pouch of Noah's binder. Here's to Myles telling me his one fun fact: he's selling fidget spinners, Fidget Cubes, and Rubik's Cubes at lunch. Here's to mediating a conflict with a co-ed quartet of study skills students who couldn't stop poking holes in their shirts and doodling on their jeans. Here's to confiscating a glue stick and finding a note hidden inside the barrel: "TRUTH: If you HAD to French kiss Jason or Jesús, who would you pick and why?" Here's to sitting down at my desk after the final bell and reading the message I got from a counselor during lunch: *Is Pacey distracted when talking to you 1:1 or with any of his peers? Is he talking to himself in class? Is he talking to his binder which he has named "Binder"?*

Here's to the boys and girls with speech impediments, activity limitations, spectrum abilities, and other labeled and unlabeled preteen gifts. Here's to Logan comparing his two loving mothers to a self-driving car: "weird, awesome, and just not popular yet." Here's to the girl talking to her friend outside my door—"Today's your birthday? That's so cool!"—and to young people who still love folding notebook paper into fortune tellers, ninja stars, and inflatable sweet rice dumplings when they should be writing.

Here's to the students who have an appreciation for the whole story. Here's to Kaya staying after class to tell me about mixing an elixir in her backyard to kill an evil doctor rat and free the water fairies.

Here's to you. May you continue to mystify me, sometimes without knowing it, sometimes knowing it a little, and sometimes knowing it all.

Epilogue

The Summer after the First Year

Carl's truck rumbles over the hill. The bluegrass grows low on the ground. Dust spins over the fields. Part-time seasonal labor attracts the kind of people who are available to work, so when Carl slows, six high-school kids, three college kids, two women who live down the road, and two guys in their twenties—including me—grab a hoe from the back.

Every worker claims a spot by setting a water thermos at the end of the row. Our work is to uproot anything other than bluegrass. We play twenty questions and hinky pinky to pass the time. Last week, we spent two days pondering nature metaphors. Kacey said she's like a cicada, underground and silent for thirteen years and emerging in an explosion of climbing and flying and courting.

"Then you die?"

"That would be the way," she said.

I said I liked sand bubbler crabs for the way they rummage through dirt for nutrients.

The pace of conversation follows the work. When we reach the end of one row we turn around and start the next. Yesterday Carl asked me a question just as the sun's fingers were moving from my shoulders to my neck.

"How's teaching?" he asked.

"What about it?"

"Wasn't this your first year?"

I looked at a hill in the distance. "Well, that's a question for the Question Jar. There was a fair amount of NyQuil and a kid named Mason," I said. "You wouldn't believe some of the stuff he came up with. Amazing kid. He could tell this story better than anyone."

When the sun shines straight above us and our shadows disappear, the morning shift ends, and we go back the way we came. I've spent the last few afternoons reading *The Odyssey* and writing letters to Idaho Girl. I wouldn't call it an "explosion of courting." Like the work I do on the farm each day, I pick up where I left off the day before. I also followed Megan's mix CD rule and wrote her a letter. She wrote back. "I like your typewriter paper," she wrote. "Are the sheets in a pile with the pages attached to each other, like how you described Jack Kerouac? That's what I envision." She moved on to continue the conversation about the CD.

I agree with almost everything you said about the songs. Number 2 makes me sway blissfully. When I hear this song, I feel like I have all the meaning in the world inside of my body. This goes along with what you said about this song being for people who feel deeply. Addendum to number 6: I love the way her "er" turns into "AW!" like "leader" becomes "leadAW!" Re: number 9, you're right that I wrote it. I'm proud of the sounds I made, and I picture the birds doing the chirping each time I listen. I'm mostly proud that I created such birds. Don't worry about the birds being caged, Mr. Smith. I created the birds to be in a big room that is the world.

What am I working on? I guess I'm always working on being extremely knowledgeable about politics and literature and on shedding the part of my self-awareness that is too keen. The part of me that's oblivious is the part of me that likes to dream. Is it like that for you? My obliviousness lets me do things like lie on the bench by the loop where the buses drop kids off during the school year and do nothing but look at the sky.

Megan

I've been dreaming too. I rewrote my freshman English course description. I began by looking up the description provided by the district: *Students are expected to learn and apply reading, writing, oral, and collaborative strategies to their own learning styles, strengths, and weaknesses.*

This is not my story.

Where is Mason's comic if occasionally absurd imagination? Where's Megan's mesmeric figurative language, describing a horse dipping its head to the ground like a spoon plunging into a bowl of soup? Where's the journey documented by pages taped together in an endless stream, like Jack Kerouac?

Freshman English returns students to old human skills like talking about books and using pencils to tell stories. By reading on a regular basis, students consider new perspectives and ways of living. By writing on a regular basis, students develop calluses on their middle fingers. As calluses thicken, students downgrade from pencils to fountain pens. Mastering fountain pens, they try feathers and reeds. Everyone writes on Megan's homemade papyrus at some point.

By the end of the year, students express satisfaction with skills cultivated as a result of writing infinite drafts of poems they would never dare call "complete." They know the work is ongoing. They know to tread lightly on the journey because the journey is itself the final exam and, like most exams, requires the strength of stone.

Acknowledgments

Thank you to Amy Bloch, Taylor Buck, Kurt Carino, Ian Clark, James Enebrad, Drew Hansen, Sarah Hiraki, Nick Markman, Reno Sorensen, and Micaela Wakefield for letting me use excerpts of their writing. Thank you also to Kurt Carino, Nakee McGary, Nhu-San Nguyen, and Zitlaly Valeriano, who are quoted as themselves. The inspirational teachers described in "The Night before the First Day" are also quoted as themselves. All other names, and some identifying details, have been changed.

To my mentor teachers: Thank you for filling three-inch binders with observations about my student teaching. Thank you for asking me difficult questions and waiting silently for answers. I learned more about teaching from you than from anyone, and I have yet to hear of a student teaching experience like mine.

Additionally, my appreciation goes to friends, former students, family members, and colleagues who offered feedback: Patrick Renie, James Boutin, Ehren Gossler, Heidi Lally, Jordan Hartt, Betsy Kalman, Michael Colasurdo, Lucia Vojtech, Elizabeth Duffey, Banyon McBrayer, Maria Kuffel, Lindsey DeLoach, Nova Gattman, David Jacobsen, Ross Gale, Kolby Kerr, Elizabeth Stewart, Erin Felton, and Andrew Shutes-David.

Thank you to the folks at Les Schwab for fixing my tires.

Steven Didis designed the cover, and Dan'l Linehan designed the website. Thank you for your efforts and your eyes.

I am indebted to any author who writes about teaching with a balance of sentimentality and realism. I have great admiration for Jonathan Kozol (*Death at an Early Age: The Destruction of the Hearts and Minds of Negro Children in the Boston Public Schools*), Esmé Raji Codell (*Educating Esmé: Diary of a Teacher's First Year*), Frank McCourt (*Teacher Man: A Memoir*), and Tracy Kidder (*Among Schoolchildren*). Thank you to LouAnne Johnson for writing *My Posse Don't Do Homework*, and for returning the royalty check from the *Dangerous Minds* television show uncashed when your TV character hosted a fundraiser in a strip club. Thank you for insisting on the humanity and complexity of teachers and students alike, and for taking the time to write me.

Thank you to all my friends, and to all my family, and to my entire network of educators, for listening to me talk about this book for eight years and for respecting the work of teachers.

Thank you, Bret Lott, for making sure Justin's hat, headphones, and hoodie were on his head in the right order. Thank you, Leslie Leyland Fields, for asking me about the mistakes I made as a new teacher. Thank you, Heidi, for encouraging me to begin.

Thank you, Michael, for being the brightest littlest thing.

About the Author

Derek Smith lives in Seattle, Washington, where he teaches English and writes about education, faith, gender, and place. He has taught high school, middle school, and college for fifteen years.

Made in the
USA
Monee, IL